Series Editor: Neville Grant

Classroom Testing

J. B. Heaton

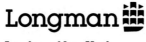

London   New York

Longman Group UK Limited,
Longman House, Burnt Mill, Harlow,
Essex CM20 2JE, England
and Associated Companies throughout the world.

Published in the United States of America
by Longman Inc., New York

© Longman Group UK Limited 1990

First published 1990
Third impression 1990

British Library Cataloguing in Publication Data
Heaton, J.B.
    Classroom testing – (Longman keys to language teaching).
    1. Educational institutions. Students. Modern language
    I. Title
    418'.007

Library of Congress Cataloging in Publication Data
Heaton, J.B. (John Brian)
    Classroom testing/J.B. Heaton.
        p.   cm. – (Longman keys to language teaching)
    1. English language – Study and teaching – Foreign speakers.
2. English language - Ability testing.   I. Title.   II. Series.
PE1128.A2H386   1989
418'.0076—dc20

Set in 10/12pt Linotron 202 Century Schoolbook roman
Produced by Longman Group (FE) Ltd
Printed in Hong Kong

ISBN 0582 74625.6

Author's acknowledgements
For my friends and colleagues at the University of
Cambridge Local Examinations Syndicate and the
Instituto Cultural Anglo-Uruguayo, Montevideo

Acknowledgements
We are grateful to the following for permission to
reproduce copyright material:

Cassell Ltd, R. Knight, *Writing 2 (1986),* for the line
drawing on page 64. Longman Group UK Ltd, J.B.
Heaton, *Beginning Composition Through Pictures*, for
two illustrations on page 63.

Contents

Preface

THE *Longman Keys to Language Teaching* series is intended especially for ordinary teachers. The books in the *Keys* series offer realistic, practical, down-to-earth advice on useful techniques and approaches in the modern ELT classroom. Most of the activities suggested in these books can be adapted and used for almost any class, by any teacher.

One of the subjects of most concern to all teachers is classroom testing. For what reasons should we do it? How should we do it? How often should we do it? How should we organise it? Can it be harmful? What is the relationship between teaching and testing? These are just some of the questions that Brian Heaton addresses in this book. With a minimum of jargon, a number of fundamental concepts are treated in a highly accessible manner.

As well as a discussion of these important issues, the author includes a great many examples of tests that teachers can adapt and use in their own classrooms. In addition, he gives valuable advice on the role of continuous assessment, in which there has been an increasing amount of interest in recent years. The book also contains some very helpful suggestions on oral testing – including how to cope with this in large classes.

This book is organised slightly differently from the other titles in the *Keys* series. At the end of each chapter there is a very useful Activities section, in which the reader is invited to evaluate different kinds of tests, and/or to formulate similar tests for their own students. This is then followed by a Discussion section, which relates the activities to the issues raised in the chapter. As a result, teachers will find that this book can have immediate applications in their own classrooms.

Neville Grant

Introduction

Writing classroom tests

This book shows you how to write useful tests for use in the classroom. Certain test papers and books at present in use in schools contain badly written questions which have a harmful effect on learning English. For example, an excessive use of multiple-choice tests of grammar may hinder students' progress rather than help it.

The most useful tests for use in the classroom are those tests which you write yourself. Only you know your students, the work you have done with your class, your students' strengths and weaknesses, and the skills and areas of language you wish to emphasise both in your teaching and in your testing. As a result, even the best book of tests will not be as suitable for your class as the tests you write specially for your purpose.

Two basic principles

Every test should be **reliable**. In other words, a test should measure precisely whatever it is supposed to measure. If a group of students were to take the same test on two occasions, their results should be roughly the same – provided that nothing has happened in the interval (such as one student receiving private tuition or several students comparing notes and specially preparing for the test when it is set a second time). Thus if students' results are very different (e.g. the top student scoring low marks the second time), the test cannot be described as reliable.

Sometimes a test can be unreliable because of the way it is marked. For example, if an average composition is marked immediately after a very good composition, the average composition may be given a mark which is actually below average. The marker's subconscious comparison of the two compositions will result in the average composition appearing worse than it really is. However, if the same average composition is marked immediately after a very poor composition, then it may appear above average and be awarded a higher mark than it deserves.

Finally, different markers may award different marks to the same composition; for example, some of the markers may be very lenient and others may be unfairly strict.

Every test should also be **valid**. A test should measure whatever it is supposed to measure *and nothing else.* A composition test which requires students to write about modern methods of transport may not be valid since it will measure not only an ability to write in English but also an interest in, or a knowledge of, modern transport. When students are given an oral interview, is it only their language abilities that are being assessed or are such assessments influenced by the students' personalities?

Words of caution

Many teachers and students think that exam and test scores can never be wrong. However, this is simply not the case. Every test score is surrounded by an area of uncertainty. For example, some students may not be on their best form when taking a test. Moreover, the questions in the test may favour certain students but not others.

Consequently, while a student's score on a good test will result in a fairly accurate assessment, there will always be a slight degree of uncertainty about it. We can usually be sure, of course, about the difference in performance between a student who has scored 60 per cent and one who has scored only 40 per cent. However, we cannot be as certain about the difference in performance between a student who has scored 49 per cent and one who has scored 51 per cent. If the pass–fail mark on the test happens to be 50 per cent, it then becomes very easy to fail a student who may deserve to pass or to pass a student who really should fail. As a result, crucial decisions affecting students may rest on extremely small or chance differences in test scores.

For this reason, it is always useful to take into account a number of test scores or other factors whenever an important decision is to be made about a student's ability in English. These other factors may consist of an interview with the student or an examination of the student's work in class (e.g. exercises, homework assignments and project work). The importance of continuous assessment will be dealt with later in this book.

To sum up in the meantime, however, it is advisable to treat all test scores with caution. There is no such thing as a perfect test.

Discussion

1 Do you write your own tests or do you use books of tests on your course? Do those students who are best at using English always score the highest marks on these tests? Why/Why not?

2 Were you ever surprised when a good student scored a low mark in an exam or a test? Can you give any explanation for this?

3 Do you ever assess your students by means other than classroom tests? If so, what other means do you use and how often do you do this?

Reasons for testing

Finding out about progress

The type of test we give will depend very much on our purpose in testing. There are many reasons for giving a test, of course, and we should always ask ourselves about the real purpose of the test which we are giving to our students. Perhaps the most important reason is to find out how well the students have mastered the language areas and skills which have just been taught. These tests look *back* at what students have achieved and are called progress tests. Class progress tests are usually the most important kinds of tests for teachers.

Also, unlike most other kinds of tests, progress tests should produce a cluster of high marks. If we test what has recently been taught and practised (possibly over the past few days or weeks), then we should expect students to score fairly high marks. If most of the students fail to score high marks, something must have been wrong with the teaching, the syllabus or the materials. Consequently, we would expect to see most of the students' marks concentrated around 80 per cent or 90 per cent rather than spread out widely from 0 per cent to 100 per cent.

A regular programme of progress tests is useful as it can help to emphasise certain language skills which might otherwise be ignored on a particular course. It also acts as a safeguard against hurrying on to complete a syllabus or textbook regardless of what the students are actually achieving – or failing to achieve.

Although you should try to give progress tests regularly, you should avoid over-testing. Too many progress tests can have as harmful an effect on students' attitudes to learning as none at all. Moreover, progress tests should be given as informally as possible. The best progress test is one which students do not recognise as a test but see as simply an enjoyable and meaningful activity.

Because you will set out in a progress test to assess what you have recently taught, you should be careful to avoid encouraging rote learning in students. Once students suspect that your test is limited to what you have just taught, many will be tempted to learn by heart various language patterns, etc. Consequently, you should write questions which lead to students *applying* what they have learnt. Above all, take care to avoid using the same material for testing that you have been using for teaching. Instead, use different material covering the same language areas and different texts containing similar features or involving similar tasks.

Encouraging students

An important function of teacher-made tests is to encourage students. Learning English is not like learning a subject such as geography or general science. In these latter two subjects we can easily measure our progress by asking ourselves what we have learned in terms of facts and figures. However, this is not the case with learning a foreign language, and it is often very difficult indeed for us to judge our own progress. At first when we start learning a foreign language, we appear to make very good progress and we are filled with enthusiasm. Later, however, we find it extremely difficult to see any progress at all and we lose our initial enthusiasm – even though we may actually be making steady progress all the time.

A classroom test can help to show students the progress which they are undoubtedly making. It can serve to show them each set of goals which they have reached on their way to fluency. Indeed, such a test would be used for the purpose of increasing motivation, yielding good results similar to those shown in the previous section.

Most people like the things they are good at – or, possibly, they are usually good at the things which they like. Obviously there are weaknesses in such generalisations, but at least it can be claimed that there is usually some connection between liking something and being good at it.

Finding out about learning difficulties

In our teaching, we may sometimes be tempted to concentrate on following the syllabus and ignore the needs of our students. However, if we do this, a lot of our students may fail however thoroughly we have covered the syllabus. It is very important to take into account the needs of our students at every stage in our teaching. Just as it is necessary for doctors to diagnose an illness in order to cure their patients, so teachers must diagnose problems in order to teach effectively.

A good diagnostic test helps us to check our students' progress for specific weaknesses and problems they may have encountered. In order to find out what these weaknesses are, we must be systematic when we design our test. In short, we should know exactly what we are testing.

We do not usually want to assess the student's ability to handle everything in the syllabus. This would be far too ambitious and in any case would deter the student. We must select areas where we think there are likely to be problems or weaknesses.

Certain kinds of tests are not as suitable for diagnostic testing as others. For example, it is more difficult to use a skills test such as a reading test or test of free writing to determine problem areas in a systematic way – although it must be emphasised that such tests can be used for diagnostic purposes. Certain tests of grammar and pronunciation, on the other hand, are reasonably straightforward for use in diagnosing students' difficulties.

Usually a diagnostic test forms part of another type of test, especially a classroom progress test. As such, it is useful to regard diagnostic testing as an ongoing part of the teaching and testing process. It is usually an integral part of a programme of continuous assessment. However, we may sometimes wish to diagnose students' difficulties before a course begins (in a proficiency or placement test) or towards the end of a course (in an achievement test).

When we mark a diagnostic test, we should try to identify and group together a student's marks on particular areas of language. For example, if we have set a grammar test, we should put the marks scored on all the items in one grammatical area together. The following shows the performance of one student on a grammar test. (Note that only ten questions are shown in this example. In order to diagnose weaknesses reliably, however, we would need to set at least forty or fifty questions. The principle of using a test for diagnosing difficulties, however, remains exactly the same.)

Specimen grammar test

1 I'll see you tomorrow __at__ ten o'clock. ✓

2 Sue and Dave __live__ here for over a year. ✗

3 __The happiness__ is more important than money. ✗

4 Can you guess who I __saw__ yesterday? ✓

5 That's the person __who__ called yesterday. ✓

6 Is there a chemist's shop __beside__ the bank? ✓

7 Mr Law gave ten dollars to the fund for __a poor__. ✗

8 I scored 9 __out of__ 10 on the test. ✓

9 Mr and Mrs Dobson __have left__ an hour ago. ✗

10 Is that the girl __of whom__ pen you borrowed? ✗

Correct answers

1 at	6 beside
2 have lived	7 the poor
3 Happiness (without *the*)	8 out of
4 saw	9 left
5 who	10 whose

Marks (Grouped together)	**Score**
Prepositions (Q1, 6, 8):	3/3
Tenses (Q2, 4, 9):	1/3
Articles (Q3, 7):	0/2
Relative pronouns (Q5, 10):	1/2

```
Diagnosis
    Prepositions:  no problems
         Tenses:  problems with present perfect v present
                  simple contrast and with present perfect
                  v past simple contrast
        Articles:  problems with articles before
                  uncountable (abstract) nouns and before
                  adjectives used as nouns to signify
                  groups: e.g. the blind, the young
Relative pronouns:  some problems e.g. who, of whom
```

It is not necessary to confine diagnostic tests to tests of grammar, of course. We can use tests in a similar way to diagnose difficulties in handling functions, notions and various concepts as well as difficulties involving language skills and sub-skills.

Diagnostic tests of all kinds are essential if we wish to *evaluate* our teaching. We can also evaluate the syllabus, the course book and the materials we are using. Problems and difficulties may arise because a particular area of language or a certain sub-skill has been glossed over in the course book or because we have not provided students with enough practice. Whatever the reason, a classroom test can enable us to locate difficulties and to plan appropriate remedial teaching.

Before we leave the subject of diagnostic testing, it should be emphasised that it will hardly be necessary for us to plan remedial teaching for the whole class if only two or three students have difficulty with a particular grammatical feature or aspect of language. If, however, as many as a quarter or a third of the class have difficulty, it becomes essential to identify the reason and give additional teaching.

Finding out about achievement

Most people associate testing with achievement or attainment tests. Unfortunately, too many people think these tests are the chief – or only – type of test. This is not the case. Unfortunately, the use of achievement tests sometimes demonstrates a more negative (but essential) side of testing.

In certain ways an achievement test is also like a progress test but it is usually designed to cover a longer period of learning than a progress test. Unlike progress tests, achievement tests should attempt to cover as much of the syllabus as possible. If we confine our test to only part of the syllabus, the contents of the test will not reflect all that has been learned.

An achievement test is usually a formal examination, given at the end of the school year or at the end of the course. Often it takes the form of an external test which is set by an examining body: e.g. the University of Cambridge Local Examinations Syndicate, the Royal Society of Arts, the Test of English as a Foreign Language (TOEFL).

A test of achievement measures a student's mastery of what should have been taught (but not necessarily what has actually been taught). It is thus concerned with covering a sample (or selection) which accurately represents the contents of a syllabus or a course book.

Informal attainment tests measure mastery of what has been learned over the past term or year. These tests are usually set by the class teacher.

If you set an achievement test for several classes as well as your own class, you should take care to avoid measuring what you yourself have taught – otherwise you will favour your own class. By basing your test on the syllabus or course book rather than on your teaching, your test will be fair to students in all the classes being tested. In this way, you will be able to establish and maintain a certain standard each year, regardless of individual teachers and classes.

Problems of knowing what to include in the test (i.e. sampling) may sometimes arise in designing an achievement test because there is often so much ground to cover. We may thus find it difficult to know what to leave out of the test and what to put in. For example, if students have been learning English for five years, how much of their earlier mastery of the language should we test?

Finally, it is important to emphasise here the value of close cooperation with colleagues. Getting together with other teachers can make the writing of good achievement tests a lot easier. Indeed, such team work will improve all the various kinds of tests you may want to write.

Placing students

A placement test enables us to sort students into groups according to their language ability at the beginning of a course. Such a test should be as general as possible and should concentrate on testing a wide and representative range of ability in English. It should thus avoid concentrating on narrow areas of language and specific skills. Consequently, questions measuring general language ability can form a useful part of a placement test. These questions often consist of blank-filling items and tests of dictation.

Such questions, however, should make up only one part of a placement test. The most important part of the test should consist of questions directly concerned with the specific language skills which students will require on their course. Consequently, it is important to write questions which concentrate on those skills and areas of language on which the early part of the future course concentrates. For example, it scarcely matters how well a student performs on a test of reading stories in English if the course concentrates solely on the listening and speaking skills. Nor does it matter how well a student can write informal letters to friends if the course is concerned with the use of English for study purposes.

It is thus essential to examine the syllabus very carefully and to bear it in mind constantly while writing a placement test. In this way, a placement test looks *forward* to the language demands which will be made on students during their course. Thus, for example, if students are going to learn about ways of using the past perfect tense to talk about past events, we should include items on the past simple tense (and possibly the present perfect tense) in our test as mastery of these areas will clearly be important before the past perfect tense is taught. Similarly, if students are going to be taught how to describe processes in making things, we should include questions on the passive voice in our test. In Chapter 2 we shall look in much greater detail at how to use a syllabus to design our tests.

Finally, a placement test should try to spread out the students' scores as much as possible. In this way, it is possible to divide students into several groups according to their various ability levels.

Selecting students

We may use a test to select certain candidates for a job or for a place on a course. A selection test is necessary when there are far more candidates than the number of jobs or places which are available. The purpose of the test, therefore, is to compare the performances of all the candidates and select only the best. In such a situation we are interested not so much in how well candidates can use English but in how much better than the other candidates they are. Thus a very good candidate may not be selected simply because there are even better candidates who have taken the same test. Conversely, we may have to select a fairly weak candidate because all the other candidates are very poor. We would not have selected this candidate, however, if other, better candidates had taken the test.

Norm-referenced testing

We often refer to a selection test as being *norm-referenced*. That is, we compare the performance of an individual with the other individuals in the group (i.e. the norm). Moreover, a good selection test will usually spread out students' scores over most of the scale we are using (eg from 0 per cent to 100 per cent). In this way, the results will make it easier for us to select groups of students at different levels.

> We use a norm-referenced test to show how a student's performance compares with the performances of the other students in the same group. For example, is the student in the top part of the group? Is he or she in the bottom part of the group or in the middle of the group? How many students in the group are better than the student and how many are worse?

Selection tests are rarely set by the class teacher. They are usually set by outside specialists such as public examining bodies and ministries of education. These outside specialists often draw up a syllabus or description of the test they have designed. If they do not provide a syllabus, they generally describe in some detail the objectives of their test.

Washback effect

Such examining bodies have a powerful *washback effect*. This is the phrase we use to refer to the way an exam or test influences teaching and learning in the classroom. In their attempts to enable students to pass, teachers will gear their teaching very closely indeed to the examination. If it is a good examination, it will have a useful effect on teaching; if bad, then it will have a damaging effect on teaching.

Public examining bodies themselves are usually all too aware of the influence of their examinations on teaching. For example, a few years ago in a certain country there was a serious shortage of examiners who had any real degree of oral fluency in English. As a result, it was generally agreed that any oral interview test would be very unreliable indeed since many candidates were more fluent than the examiners. Nevertheless, the examining body kept the oral interview test because it felt that no English at all would be spoken in the last year of the secondary school if the oral component were abolished!

Finding out about proficiency

We use proficiency tests to measure how suitable candidates will be for performing a certain task or following a specific course. For example, the British Council administer a proficiency test to overseas students intending to study in universities and polytechnics in Britain. This test has different parts which candidates can choose to do according to their different purposes. It is thus possible for the test to measure candidates' proficiency in certain special fields: life sciences, medicine, social studies, physical sciences, technology.

The language demands made in one subject area are usually quite different from those made in another. Thus, a candidate intending to study medicine in Britain should be given a different test from a candidate intending to study history. Consequently, most proficiency tests concentrate on assessing candidates' ability to use English for a special purpose. The candidates' general command of English may not form the chief focus for a proficiency test.

In this way, a proficiency test looks *forward* to the actual ways in which candidates will use English in the future. When you design a proficiency test, therefore, you should pay careful attention to those language areas and skills which the candidate will need. For example, if the successful candidate will work as a clerk in a commercial office in a country where English is not used for everyday communication, the test should concentrate on assessing the ability to write letters, to translate documents and possibly to read and write technical reports in English rather than an ability to write imaginative essays or hold conversations in English.

Criterion-referenced testing

In a proficiency test we are not concerned with comparing the abilities of the various candidates. We want to find out only the degree of success someone may have in doing something. Thus a proficiency test is primarily a *criterion-referenced test* – as opposed to a norm-referenced test. Quite simply, how well can the candidates perform the tasks which we give them in the test? Take the case of a garage mechanic, for example. If we have a puncture, we are interested only in knowing whether the mechanic can repair it or not – and also perhaps in how quickly or efficiently he can do it. We are not concerned at all with how well the mechanic compares with other mechanics. The same is true of our proficiency test. A comparison of scores is not our major concern, although such a comparison may, of course, add certain information for our benefit.

We use a criterion-referenced test to find out whether a student can perform a particular task or not. For example, can the student write a letter asking for information about something? Can the student give personal details about himself or herself with only occasional errors of language?

Activities

1

1 How many students in Test A have scored between 81% and 100%?
2 How many students in Test B have scored between 81% and 100%?
3 How many students in Test A have scored 60% and below?
4 What can you say about the students who have scored between 31% and 70% in Test B?
5 Which test is more successful at spreading out students' scores?

6 One of the tests shows the results of a placement test and the other the results of a progress test. Which do you think is the progress test?

Test A
Total number of students = 20 (i.e. 1+3+5+6+5 = 20)

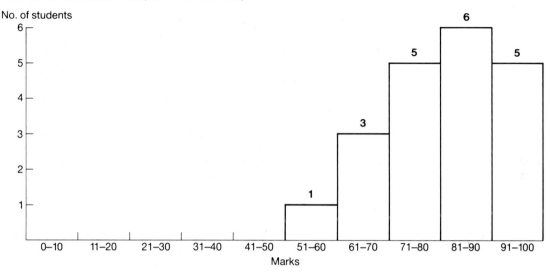

Test B
Total number of students = 20 (i.e. 1+1+2+3+3+3+3+2+1+1=20)

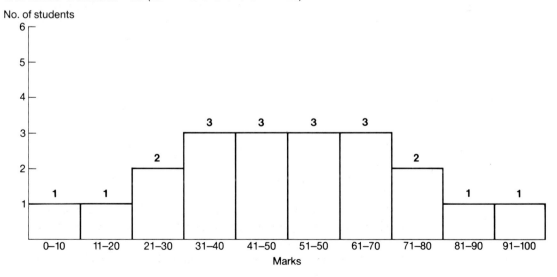

2

Read the following questions from a progress test and the students' answers. Note that there were forty students who took the test. The numbers choosing each answer are shown in brackets. Which areas would you select for remedial teaching and what would you teach?

---

(1) " _____ a competition before," he told reporters (2) _____ him. "Now 1

(3) _____ rich and I want (4) _____ my friends happy. I've got (5) _____ and I

don't need even half of it."

(1) A Never I've won *(4 students)*   C I've never won *(16 students)*
      B Have I never won *(12 students)*   D I've won never *(8 students)*

(2) A they interviewed *(3 students)*   C were interviewing *(2 students)*
      B interviewed *(1 student)*   D who interviewed *(34 students)*

(3) A become *(21 students)*   C becomes *(1 student)*
      B became *(6 students)*   D have become *(12 students)*

(4) A make *(5 students)*   C to make *(32 students)*
      B making *(1 student)*   D for making *(2 students)*

(5) A thousand dollar *(7 students)*   C thousand of dollars *(9 students)*
      B thousands dollars *(13 students)*   D thousands of dollars *(11 students)*

3

Look at the outline syllabus for the first term of a particular course which practises various skills but which concentrates on reading in English for study purposes.

Course syllabus

Theme	Function	Grammar/Structure
1 Education	Giving reasons, information, and advice	*because, because of, for* gerund & infinitive forms
2 Manufacturing	Describing processes	passive with agent
3 The environment	Talking about the future; talking about quantity	*so + adj, too + adj; enough*
4 Future trends	Making predictions; giving advice	future progressive *should, ought to*
5 Air travel	Classifying	*each, every, all, other*
6 Surveys	Reporting what others have said; understanding information in surveys	reported speech

Which of the following language skills and areas would you include in a placement test for the course described above?

Placement test

General paper: Text with blanks for completion

Reading: Vocabulary: words concerned with the cinema, schools, newspapers, sport, and food
Text: a paragraph on Shakespeare's plays
Travelling abroad by rail

Listening: A radio talk on modern music
A discussion between a husband and wife about choosing a house
A lecture on the manufacture of cloth

Writing: Grammar items on the passive voice without agent, *if* clauses, the future tense, *used to*, the past perfect continuous
Writing a formal letter of invitation to a party

Speaking: Pronunciation
Making excuses and apologising
Talking about future plans and developments

Translation

4

What language areas and activities should a proficiency test concentrate on in order to assess a candidate's suitability for each of the following? Discuss.

A job as a hotel receptionist in an international hotel
A place on a management studies course in Britain
A place on an advanced English course for scientists wishing
  to read scientific articles in English
A job as an interpreter for a large chemical company
A place as a member of a small group visiting nuclear power
  stations in the United States
A post as a research medical officer
A six-month attachment to the police in London
A place on a training course in Canada for airline pilots
A job as a nurse in a hospital in Britain
A holiday guide for English-speaking visitors to your country

---

Discussion

1 How often do you set progress tests? Do you think you do this too often or too rarely? Say why.

2 Find out how students performed in the last progress test you set. First write out the marks and then draw up a chart like those in Activities 1 on page 19.

3 What would you include in an end-of-term achievement test for your students?

4 How often do you need to give placement tests and selection tests in your own teaching situation? Are proficiency tests ever necessary? If so, for what particular purpose?

Writing and using tests

Should we write our own tests?

The answer to this question clearly depends on your own ability as a test writer and on the time which you have available. It also depends on the quality of the books and tests which you can obtain.

If you buy a book of tests, look at some of the questions very carefully and try to do a few of the tests. You will soon find out if the tests are sound and reliable for your purposes. Make sure also that the tests are at the most appropriate level for your students. Then find out whether they have been written to cover a whole year's work or to accompany a small part of a particular course.

We often buy tests to find out how our students are progressing. We want to learn about what kinds of problems our students are experiencing so that we can plan appropriate lessons or give them additional teaching.

Always remember, however, that the best tests for the classroom are those tests which you write yourself.

How often should students be tested?

This question is difficult to answer as the type of tests you set will determine how often they are given. Your reasons for testing as well as the students' own needs will also help you to determine how frequently you test your students. There is clearly a great difference between formal exams and informal classroom tests. Formal exams can generally be given to students once a year or perhaps every term at most. Such exams are usually intended to measure achievement and are used primarily to compare students' performances. Informal classroom tests, on the other hand, can be set far more frequently. These informal tests are often progress tests and are used to diagnose difficulties as well as to encourage students.

You can give classroom tests once every few weeks – sometimes even once a week. Sometimes your test may occupy an entire lesson; sometimes it may last only ten minutes or so. A short informal test of the latter type is also referred to as a quiz. It is given either at the beginning or at the end of a lesson to consolidate learning. Students' scores are not usually of primary importance in short tests of this nature since the test itself is seen as an important part of the learning process: its chief purpose is for you to check what students have learnt. If a number of students in your class make the same errors or encounter the same problems in the test, then your sole concern will lie with the relevant aspects of your teaching or the materials you are using.

Good classroom tests should always reflect the teaching that has taken place beforehand. It can be assumed in most cases, therefore, that the oral skills will be tested just as much as the written skills. If a classroom test contains only a written component and no oral component, its effect on teaching and learning can be very harmful indeed. Although oral tests can be time-consuming, regular assessments of speaking ability can be made by the teacher at any time while students are engaged in a particular activity. One of the sections in Chapter 7 shows ways in which oral testing can best be carried out.

Even informal classroom tests, however, can disrupt learning rather than encourage it if they are set too frequently. This is particularly true if they are given to the class in a tense and formal atmosphere. Consequently, always try to make sure that your students do not feel anxious when you give them the test. Don't give the impression to your students that you are assessing them every time you give them a classroom test. Remember that students' performances and abilities will not normally vary greatly (nor even noticeably) from week to week. For example, a student who is near the top of the class one week will not be near the bottom of the class the following week. If there is such variation, there is something wrong either with the test or with the student's personal circumstances. There is certainly little need for a test to provide this kind of information.

In addition, make sure that your test is enjoyable as well as useful. A good classroom test is one which students actually enjoy doing and do not regard as being a test. Remember that stimulating material can reinforce learning, whether used as part of your teaching or your testing.

One test of listening comprehension given recently required students to listen to instructions and draw a picture. As the students listened and built up their picture, they found that the instructions and their picture were in fact telling a story. After the test, students approached their teacher and pleaded with her to give them a similar test the next day!

Unfortunately, a lot of tests are harmful because they create anxiety in students. An advantage of short informal tests given frequently is that they help students to overcome such feelings of anxiety. Moreover, if the class teacher is the test writer, students will soon become familiar with the type of test usually set and will feel reassured because the test contents will be based on the course contents.

In any case, your evaluation of your students will be based on a number of tests rather than on just one. Thus, a poor result on a single test will not do too much serious damage to a student.

Drawing up a test framework

It is much more difficult to decide what to include in an English test than in, say, a test of geography. In a test of geography, for instance, you can easily describe the body of knowledge which you are testing. From your test, you can find out exactly how much a student knows about a particular geographical topic. In a test of English, it is more difficult to determine not only the precise language skills you wish to test but also the extent to which a student can perform those skills.

A teaching syllabus is of great help in designing a classroom progress test or test of achievement. You should always try to select a representative sample of skills and language areas from your syllabus or from what you have actually taught. However, you will always be faced with the question about how well students have mastered this syllabus. In other words, you will have to make a judgement about what constitutes satisfactory progress and what constitutes unsatisfactory progress.

If you do not have a syllabus, make a note of the grammar and vocabulary points (and, if possible, the communicative functions) which your coursebook has covered. Then look at the skills. What tasks are students required to perform in their reading? For example, must they be able to read quickly to obtain the gist of a text? Or should they be able to use an index? Should they be able to read intensively and to make notes of key points? If your students are at a much lower level of English, should they be able to follow a short sequence of events or to understand straightforward processes or to understand simple descriptions? In writing, what kinds of letters should students be able to write? To whom? About what subject? For what purpose?

Test construction is a very good discipline in this respect, for it forces teachers to look far more closely at both their short-term and long-term goals, especially the former. Often in our teaching, we feel we are doing good work when we teach an enjoyable lesson – even if we later feel the lesson may not have been very useful. The personalities and abilities of some teachers are so good that they can sometimes be successful by teaching lessons which do not reflect the objectives of a course.

Before you start to write your test, decide on what you want to include in it. If you want to write a short classroom test to find out how much grammar your students have revised or learned over the past few weeks, follow these steps:

1 Write down all the grammar points and structures taught and practised over the period:

> defining relative pronoun *that* (subject and object)
> *for/by* + *-ing* form
> verb (*need, begin*, etc.) + *to* infinitive
> *was born* + year
> verb (*like, hate*, etc.) + *-ing* form
> *too* + adjective (*busy*, etc.) + *to* infinitive
> present perfect tense + *for/since* time phrase
> *more/less/fewer* + count/mass nouns

2 Now give a percentage mark to each point of grammar or structure according to a) how important you feel it is in this part of the course and b) how long you have spent teaching or practising this particular area.

defining relative pronoun *that* (subject and object)	10%
for/by + *-ing* form	5%
verb (*need, begin,* etc.) + *to* infinitive	10%
was born + year	5%
verb (*like, hate,* etc.) + *-ing* form	20%
too + adjective (*busy,* etc.) + *to* infinitive	15%
present perfect tense + *for/since* time phrase	30%
more/less/fewer + count/mass nouns	20%

3 Don't worry if the total is not 100 per cent. In this case, it is 115 per cent. The aim of this procedure is simply to give you some idea of how important you regard each grammar point compared with the other grammar points you have taught. If you want to make the total reach 100 per cent, simply deduct a few percentage marks from certain selected areas. For example, you might reduce each of the following by 5 per cent (totalling 15 per cent):

verb (*like, hate,* etc.) + *-ing* form
present perfect tense + *for/since* time phrase
more/less/fewer + count/mass nouns

4 When you write the test, simply make sure that you have the appropriate proportion of each type of grammar or structure item. If your test consists of only twenty items, for example, you will have the following numbers of items for each area:

defining relative pronoun *that* (subject and object)	2 items
for/by + *-ing* form	1 item
verb (*need, begin,* etc.) + *to* infinitive	2 items
was born + year	1 item
verb (*like, hate,* etc.) + *-ing* form	3 items
too + adjective (*busy,* etc.) + *to* infinitive	3 items
present perfect tense + *for/since* time phrase	5 items
more/less/fewer + count/mass nouns	3 items

If you wish to draw up your list of specifications in terms of a functional approach, the procedure would be exactly the same. However, the list might appear as follows:

asking for information about someone	10%
giving personal information about oneself	20%
describing people	25%
expressing likes and dislikes about people	20%
making suggestions	15%
expressing preferences	10%

Note that in this latter type of test we would not wish to write individual items, but test the functions in general terms: for example, perhaps in conversations and in informal letters. Nevertheless, our list would not only serve to make us constantly aware of what we were testing but it would also enable us to give appropriate emphasis to each function.

You can also list the various skills in a similar way. The following list shows a breakdown of reading skills selected for inclusion in a particular test, together with an indication of the weighting given to each skill. In this case, the percentages cannot always be translated directly into numbers of items but they nevertheless provide a useful indication of the relative importance of the skills being tested.

deducing words from contextual clues	10%
understanding relations between parts of a text through a) reference devices and b) connectives	10%
recognising key information	20%
understanding cause-and-effect relationships	10%
drawing conclusions	10%
making simple inferences	15%
scanning to locate information	25%

Task-based testing

So far we have dealt with tests designed to measure mastery of the language without taking into account any particular use to which it may be put. We have been largely concerned with students' control of English – their ability to use tenses, articles and prepositions, etc.

We should also consider how well a student can actually perform certain tasks using English. Tests which seek to measure this ability are generally referred to as *task-based tests* (sometimes called *performance-referenced tests*). These tests attempt to answer such questions as the following: Can students understand and deal with messages in English over the telephone? Can they operate a cassette recorder using written instructions in English? Can they use a dictionary to find out the meanings of new words? Can they complete an application form for a visa? Can they persuade someone in English to buy a second-hand car?

If we try to measure these abilities by direct observation by means of task-based tests, our tests will usually be both uneconomical and impracticable. Consequently, most task-based tests are written to measure performance in an indirect way. The tasks contained in an indirect task-based test are analysed, and the skills required for those tasks are identified and selected for inclusion in the test. For example, a telephone conversation might be recorded and given as a basis for a true/false listening comprehension test. The ability to arrange in the correct sequence a set of instructions for operating a cassette recorder (or for any other similar task) might be tested. A role play involving an attempt to persuade someone to buy something might form part of an oral test. Other tasks, of course, would require fewer changes from direct testing to indirect testing. A dictionary extract might be included in a test so that students could complete gaps in sentences with the most appropriate words. An application form might be given, together with suitable instructions.

A student's performance on such task-based tests enables us to predict the student's ability to perform the same tasks in real life. We can make such predictions with far greater confidence than we can if we use the results of a test which measures only mastery of the language without any reference to its use for any particular purpose. However, we cannot use a task-based test to generalise about other aspects of the student's performance. For example, we cannot tell how well a student can write a composition or a business letter in English solely from the student's ability to complete an application form.

On the other hand, if we use a test of language mastery (i.e. of general listening, speaking, reading and writing skills or of grammar, vocabulary and phonology), we will be in a better position to make generalisations about the student's probable ability to use English for a variety of purposes.

Moreover, apart from those teachers who teach English for specific purposes (e.g. English for medicine, English for engineering, English for business), the majority of teachers will write tests for students who have very general (and often ill-defined) needs. Such teachers will not be in a position to identify many particular tasks which students may later be required to perform. Nevertheless, it is useful at times to set task-based tests in order to remind students of the importance of being able to perform certain appropriate tasks with the language they are learning (e.g. listen to a radio talk in English, use a train timetable in English, give an English-speaking tourist directions, write a letter ordering a book from Britain, etc.).

A good achievement test, therefore, will usually test both mastery of the language and the ability to perform certain everyday tasks in English.

Objective and subjective testing

We shall now use the word *item* for very short test questions (e.g. 1i) in the example which follows) and the word *question* for a number of similar items grouped together (e.g. the whole of 1 in the example). An *objective* item can be marked very quickly and completely reliably. Because an objective item has only one correct answer or a limited number of correct answers, this kind of test can be marked by a machine or by an inexperienced person. Objective items have consequently become very popular in many countries.

The following are four examples of objective questions. The questions consist of multiple-choice items (no. 1), true/false items (no. 2), ordering or re-arrangement (no. 3), and matching (no. 4). (Note that Questions 1 and 4 test control of the language whereas Questions 2 and 3 test an ability to perform particular tasks.)

1 Read the conversation below. Put a circle round the letter of the correct word to use in each blank.

i) David: Are there any good _____ on television tonight?
  A showings B programmes C screens D performances

ii) Linda: Yes, there's a very good _____ about life in the Arctic.
  A news B service C documentary D attraction

iii) *etc.*

2 Look at the following train timetable. Use the information in the timetable and write T or F after each of the sentences below it.

			Leeds – London		Mondays to Saturdays			
		MF		*MF*	*S*		*S*	*MF*
dep	0645	0725	0740	0845	0910	0945	1030c	1045
arr	0908	0945	1014	1112	1319	1312	1456	1312

dep = depart arr = arrive
c = cheap fare MF = Monday to Friday S = Saturday only

i) The first train to London on a Saturday leaves Leeds at quarter to seven _____

ii) The nine-ten train runs only on Saturdays _____

iii) *etc.*

3 The following ten sentences are about a fire drill. However, they are in the wrong order. Write the sentences in the correct order.

A Then the class should walk quickly along the corridor to the main entrance.
B Each class monitor should then check the attendance.
C *etc.*

4 Choose the best reply in List B for each sentence in List A Write the letter in the blank.

List A		List B
Good evening, sir.	_____	A Just a glass of water.
Is this table all right?	_____	B Rice, please.
Anything to drink, sir?	_____	C Yes, it's fine.
Here's the menu.	_____	D Good evening. A table for one.
Potatoes or rice with it?	_____	E Some bread, please.
Anything else, sir?	_____	F Thanks. I'd like fish.

Examples of subjective questions, on the other hand, are: compositions, reports, letters, answers to comprehension questions using students' own words, conversations, discussions (problem-solving tasks, etc.), talks (describing pictures, telling stories, etc.)

Clearly, subjective questions offer better ways of testing language skills and certain areas of language than objective questions. Since subjective questions allow for much greater freedom and flexibility in the answers they require, they can only be marked by a competent marker or teacher. Often there is no answer which is 100 per cent right or 100 per cent wrong. Markers have to use their own judgements when they award marks.

The following example shows how difficult marking subjective questions sometimes is. The question is one which you might ask a student in an oral interview; the answers are fairly typical of those which students might give.

What's your favourite pastime?

A's answer: Swimming.
B's answer: I am liking always the swimming.
C's answer: I like swimming a lot but I'm not very good at it.
D's answer: Swimming is my favourite game.
E's answer: I enjoy to swim.
F's answer: Swim.

How can these different answers be marked fairly so that we reward each student's ability appropriately? Clearly, we must have some guidelines before we can set about marking reliably. (For a more detailed treatment of this problem of marking, see the section 'Grading oral ability' in Chapter 4 and the 'General' section in Chapter 7.)

The following questions, on the other hand, present each problem clearly and are very easy to mark.

---

1 I _____ table-tennis a lot.   A am liking   B have liked   C like   D liking

2 I also enjoy _____.   A swim   B swimming   C to swim   D for swimming

3 Swimming is my favourite _____.   A sport   B game   C match   D leisure

There are certain times when *recognition* items like the previous ones are useful in testing grammar. Before students can learn to produce appropriate forms of language, they must first be able to recognise them. Thus such multiple-choice tests of grammar may be useful at certain stages in learning new language forms – provided that you do not think students are good at using language simply because they can recognise correct forms of language. If students are given such items too frequently in classroom tests, they will not learn how to use English. Indeed, an abundance of such questions in tests may do considerable harm.

Always remember that most good tests contain both objective and subjective types of items.

Activities

1
Comment on the following situations. How often do you think the exams and tests referred to should be given to students?

Situation A

TERM 1:	Beginning-of-term placement test (the teacher keeps a note of each student's score.)
	End-of-term exam (The teacher keeps a note of each student's score and gives a copy to the principal.)
TERM 2:	End-of-term exam (The teacher keeps a note of each student's score and gives a copy to the principal.)
TERM 3:	End-of-year practice exam (The teacher keeps a note of each student's score.)
	End-of-year exam (The teacher gives each student's score to the principal and enters the scores on a report.)

Note: All the tests and exams are written ones and consist of multiple-choice items and gap-filling items.

Situation B

> TERM 1: Every 2 weeks: class progress tests (The teacher
> keeps a note of how many students obtained each
> mark – but not of the individual students' scores.
> Usually the students exchange their test papers
> and mark them.) In addition, a ten-minute test at
> the end of the lesson at least once a week,
> concentrating on what has just been learned.
> (Again, test papers are exchanged and marked in
> class, and the teacher notes how many students
> obtained each mark.)
>
> Note: All the tests are based on what has just been taught. The
> items used in the tests vary according to the language skills
> which they are testing.

2

Read the following brief list of skills and functions which has
been drawn up to be included in a test. Write down what you
think are the most appropriate points of grammar and structure
which arise from the functions and which might be included in
another part of the same progress test.

> listening to simple directions
> having a conversation with someone about a person you both
>   know
> talking about a recent incident or experience
> reading simple descriptions of scenes
> writing a letter to a friend, suggesting you meet to see
>   a new detective film

Example: listening to simple directions

  prepositions of place (*at, in, on,* etc.)
  adverbs (*straight on,* etc.)
  imperative forms
  after/before + *-ing* form

3

A few types of questions can be classed as either objective or
subjective. Answer the following questions. Then comment on

them, saying whether you think they are objective or subjective.
Give your reasons.

---

1 Write the best word in each blank.

Dear Professor Zodiac,

    I was born on May 2nd, 1976 two minutes before noon. I should be most grateful if you could answer the following _____ .

  i) Will I change my job?

  ii) When will I get _____?

  iii) Will I travel abroad in the near future?

  iv) Will I become _____ later in my life?

Yours sincerely,

Mandy Potts

2 Write one word or more in each blank.

I _____ on my way home when I saw Anna.

I realised then that I _____ her for ages.

"Where _____?" I asked her... *etc.*

3 Complete the second sentence in each pair so that it has the same meaning as the first sentence.

a) I will lend you enough money to pay your fees.

  You can _____

b) Fortunately, the fees in this college are cheaper than those in Oxford College.

  Fortunately, the fees in this college are not _____

  _____ ... *etc.*

4 Finish the second sentence.

The weather in Britain is often very changeable.

For example, _____

_____

It is impossible to predict what it will be like from one day to another... *etc.*

5 Complete this conversation by writing A's part.

A: _____

B: I'm fine, thanks.

A: _____

B: Yes, we're going to Paris for three weeks. What about you?

A: _____

B: Oh dear, I do hope that you *will* be able to have a rest. You're working too hard! . . .
etc.

6 Read the following paragraph about future air travel. One word is missing from each line. Put an oblique stroke (/) where the word has been omitted and write the missing word in each blank.

Soon there be giant 'airports' in the sky.   1) _____

These flying 'airports' which called spanloaders   2) _____

will consist two large wings.   3) _____
etc.

Discussion

1 Study carefully a test which you or your colleagues have recently written. In what ways do you think it was a good test? In what ways was it a poor test?

2 How can you reduce students' feelings of anxiety about testing?

3 Make a list of the areas of grammar and/or functions which you would try to include in an end-of-term classroom test. Give each area of grammar or function a weighting (e.g. 15 per cent, 30 per cent, etc.).

4 What proportion of your test paper would consist of objective items? Justify this.

Testing listening skills

Distinguishing between sounds

In the early stages of learning English, your students will probably have some difficulty in actually hearing the difference between one particular sound and another: e.g. *live* and *leave, sell* and *shell, heart* and *hut*. If students have no equivalent sound in their own language, they may sometimes have serious problems. For example, the *r* sound in English (as in *raw*) does not exist in Cantonese, and thus students often tend to 'hear' the nearest equivalent in their own language: *l*. As a result, many students at first will not be able to tell the difference between *raw* and *law*. Others may be unable to hear the difference between, for example, *washing* and *watching*. In teaching and testing the ability to recognise the different sounds, it is easier to start by pronouncing the words in isolation:

washing
watching

If presented in isolation (e.g. *hill, heel; shop, chop; viper, wiper; bud, bird*; etc.), several sounds can be tested in a few minutes. However, when we do this, we tend to emphasise or exaggerate the difference between the two sounds when we pronounce them. The next step, therefore, is to say the words naturally in sentences:

The policeman's washing the car.
The policeman's watching the car.

The final consonant sound in certain words (e.g. *seventeen* not *seventy, closed* not *close*) and the use of contractions (e.g. *she'd done it* not *she done it, he's singing* not *he singing*) can also cause problems.

Again, it is usually preferable to test sound differences in a context. The following item provides an illustration of just one way in which this may be attempted.

Listen carefully to the short talk which your teacher will give. You will hear ONE of the words or phrases in each of the following pairs. You will hear it in the same order as it is listed here. Write the letter of the word or phrase.

 1 A hate   B hit
 2 A beans   B beings
 3 A not dangerous   B no danger
 4 A filling   B feeling
 5 A flows   B flies
 6 A victor   B victim
 7 A jaw   B shore
 8 A whole   B hollow
 9 A bitten   B beaten
10 A try   B tried

(Short talk to be read aloud.)

Many people hate snakes and try to kill them whenever they can. Snakes will attack human beings, however, only when they are disturbed. Did you know that a snake's tongue is not dangerous? It is simply for feeling things and smelling substances. A snake's poison flows through its fangs into the body of its victim. These fangs are in the upper jaw and are really hollow teeth. If you are bitten by a snake, keep calm, try to remember what the snake looked like and see a doctor at once.

Tests of stress and intonation are very important for inclusion in progress tests at the early levels, too. Unfortunately, however, a student may learn the correct stress patterns for certain words but still be unable to pronounce the words correctly – thus it is of little use learning to recognise word stress without being able to apply this knowledge.

Finally, it must be pointed out that items testing stress and intonation are often dull and artificial. Such 'hearing' tests should be short and used primarily for a particular teaching purpose – i.e. for developing an initial awareness of certain sounds. For most purposes, however, it is far better to concentrate on testing students' understanding of short conversations and talks in as natural a way as possible. Above all, it is important to realise that the ability to hear sound differences is not necessarily the same as the ability to understand spoken messages.

Dictation

Some teachers think of dictation chiefly as a test of spelling. Although dictation may include an assessment of spelling, it tests a wide range of skills. A dictation can also provide a useful means of measuring general language performance. Dictation is included in this chapter because it has long been closely associated with listening comprehension.

When you give a dictation to your class, begin by reading through the whole dictation passage at almost normal speed. Then dictate meaningful units of words (phrases and short clauses), reading them aloud as clearly as possible. Finally, after finishing the actual dictation of the various phrases and clauses, read the whole passage once more at slightly slower than normal speed. Students will then be given an opportunity to check the spellings of words and their overall understanding of the text.

Unfortunately, some teachers try to make the dictation easier for their students by reading out the text very slowly word by word. This way of giving dictation can be very harmful as it encourages students to concentrate on single words. It also makes it difficult for them to follow what is being dictated in this way.

Clearly, you should give students enough time to write down what you are dictating. To do this, simply pause at the end of a meaningful unit (or sense group) to allow the students time to write down what you have just read out. It is important to choose a suitable text for dictation with this in mind and to prepare beforehand by dividing the text into intelligible segments.

Every year / thousands of new words / come into the English language. // Although most of these words / disappear after a short time, / one or two hundred words / eventually find their way into the dictionary. // Who decides which words are kept? //

Marking a dictation is fairly straightforward. Usually half a mark or one mark is deducted for each error. Sometimes spelling and punctuation errors are treated less seriously than grammar errors or the insertion of other words (showing a failure to understand what has been dictated). However, for most purposes it is recommended that you deduct one mark for each mistake – say, out of a total of twenty.

It is often useful if you can give the same short text first for listening comprehension and then for dictation, especially if your test is seen as an integral part of your teaching. The following steps illustrate one method to use.

1 Read the text aloud in as natural a way as possible.

2 Ask students to answer two or three general questions on it after they have listened to your reading.

OR   Ask two or three general questions before you read the text a second time.

3 Read the text aloud for dictation (i.e. give the second reading in short, meaningful units).

4 Read the text a final time for students to check their dictation.

The following list of exercise types shows a few of the various activities you can use before the actual dictation. Remember that you should normally use only one of the activities given below.

---

1 Listen carefully to the following short talk which I shall read aloud. After you have heard it, answer the following questions:

Why was table tennis first called 'ping-pong'?
Why are rubber bats used now?

2 In the passage for dictation the following eight past tense forms and past participles are used. Listen carefully and number these in the order in which they occur.

painted   made   bought   returned
examined   went   began   gave

3 Listen carefully and write down all the numbers you hear in the talk I am about to give.

4 Listen carefully to the talk. You will hear one of the following words or phrases in each pair. Write the letter of the word or phrase.

1	A	live	B	leave
2	A	one other	B	one another
3	A	tall	B	all
4	A	2,000	B	20,000
5	A	storeys	B	stories

---

5 Listen carefully to the passage for dictation. Write the missing word in each of the following phrases:

1 to many _____ tales

2 by actually _____ the milk out of them

3 and are _____ to farmers

4 snakes choose _____ for their diet

5 according to _____ belief

Characteristics of the spoken language

Repeating information

Before we look at ways of testing listening comprehension, we should first consider what is involved in understanding the spoken language.

The spoken language contains a lot of redundancy, and meaning is usually reinforced or repeated in several ways. For example, we can tell the following is a question both by the word order (i.e. inversion of auxiliary and main verb) and by the rising intonation:

Would you care for a game of tennis?

The message can still be understood even when several words are omitted:

Care for a game of tennis?
Game of tennis?
Tennis?

Pausing

We often hesitate and pause when we speak, filling in the gaps with sounds such as *er, huh* and *em*. Sometimes we start a sentence, change our mind and then start it again:

Er ... What do you ... em ... would you care for a game of tennis?

Such false starts and hesitation features are an important part of the spoken language, actually helping us to follow what is being said. The situation also helps our understanding of this question: for example, the speaker might have a tennis racket in his or her hand or be on the way to some tennis courts.

Differences between speaking and writing

The structure of the spoken language differs from that of the written language. When we write, we organise language in sentences. When we speak, however, we generally organise language in clauses. We often connect these clauses with words like *and, but* and *so*. We seldom use complex sentences in spontaneous speech. Compare, for example, this spoken message with its written equivalent.

(Spoken) We went for *dim sum* and we'd a lot of very nice Chinese dishes not usually served in England ... er ... and after that we went ... we went to my house and Grandma had a look round and she was very impressed ... she really liked it. She thought it was a lovely house and that we should stay there and do it up. Then we went to ... er ... this mill ... erm ... and it was terribly hot – it was in the middle of a heat wave – and we saw some old machinery.

(Written) We went for *dim sum*, which consisted of numerous excellent Chinese dishes not usually served in England. After eating *dim sum*, we went to my house so that my grandmother could look round. She was so impressed by the house that she advised us to stay there and decorate it. Although it was in the middle of a heat wave, we next visited a mill, where we examined some old machinery.

What do we remember?

People remember the general meaning of a sentence rather than the actual words themselves. For example, when we hear the sentence

The train slowly rounded the bend and came to a halt a few minutes later.

we remember only that the train stopped shortly after it had slowly gone round the bend. We would simply have no idea if someone later asked us whether the speaker had said *came round* instead of *rounded, stopped* instead of *came to a halt*, or *moments* instead of *minutes*. It is the meaning and not the actual words which we normally remember.

Students sometimes feel so concerned about their inability to understand every word at the beginning of a talk in English that they become discouraged and switch off. Thus it becomes important for you to educate students, emphasising that it is not essential to understand every word in order to follow the gist of a talk and providing appropriate practice to convince them.

The importance of context

Moreover, we usually use language in a certain situation for a particular purpose. For example, spoken in isolation the sentence

Linda talked a lot

could be a criticism of Linda, a favourable comment, a denial of what has just been said or even an explanation of why the speaker had no chance to talk to Linda. Its meaning depends entirely on the context in which it is spoken.

Using recorded material

The use of eyes, facial movements and gestures when we speak is very important in helping listeners to understand the message we are giving. That is why it is always more difficult (especially for foreign speakers of a language) to understand someone talking over the telephone. It is even more difficult for learners to understand conversations and talks recorded on cassettes. Video recordings are different; we can see the person who is speaking. Cassettes, however, do not enable us to see the speaker, and thus a higher and possibly a more intense level of listening ability is often demanded.

Implications for listening tests

Talking – not reading

Always try to *talk* to students in a test of listening. Avoid reading aloud long written texts if you possibly can. As we saw in the previous section, written texts lack most of the redundant features which are so important in helping us to understand speech. Most of us have experienced how much more difficult it is to follow a lecture which is read aloud than one which is given from brief notes.

Consequently, try to give a talk from brief notes. Simply jot down the main points of your talk, making sure that you will mention every point which occurs in the written questions on the talk. Don't worry if you make any grammatical errors when you give the talk. Making mistakes is all part of using language; even native-speakers make mistakes. Avoid rehearsing your talk and learning it by heart. If you do this, your talk will be unnatural and probably uninteresting.

It is a good idea to use pictures from time to time to help you give a talk for listening comprehension. Describe a picture to the class or use a series of pictures to tell a story or to describe a process. When you do this, first look at the pictures and jot down the various points about which you will ask questions later. Then write down a brief note for each point so that you do not miss it out when you are talking.

Reading texts aloud

As we have seen, written texts omit most of the redundancy of the spoken language. Although it is easy to advise giving talks from notes (as opposed to reading the talk aloud), in practice it is usually difficult to do this in a foreign language. Some teachers may not feel confident enough to give a talk spontaneously, especially in a test situation. As a result, it is often necessary to read aloud a written text.

If you do decide to read a talk aloud, try to make the following appropriate changes to the written text first. Such changes will make up for the lack of redundancy in the written text.

1 Rewrite most of the complex sentences, making sure the sentences for reading aloud are fairly short. Use coordinating conjunctions (e.g. *and, but, or,* and *so*) instead of subordinate conjunctions (e.g. *although, whereas, in order that,* etc.).

2 Rewrite the talk, itself, and repeat the important points. Try restating these key points in different language. In this way, you will be able to emphasise what is important. At the same time, you will give students practice in recognising points which have been re-phrased.

3 When you read the written text aloud, pause slightly longer than normally at the end of clauses and sentences. Longer pauses are far better than reading the text very slowly. Indeed,

reading aloud slowly is very unnatural and sometimes makes a text more difficult to understand.

4 Finally, remember that the comprehension of a written text appears deceptively easy when you are familiar with the text and can see it in printed form. It is far different when you are listening for the first (and only) time to the text being read aloud! Try to put yourself in the position of a student listening to the text when you write questions based on the text.

Using Recordings

In the previous section, we saw that it was much harder to understand speakers if we could not see them. Thus, talks and conversations recorded on cassette tape are a much harder test of understanding than those given in real life (or those recorded on video tape).

However, cassette tape recordings have the following advantages:

1 They help to make a listening test more reliable. The same voice is heard giving the talk in exactly the same way, regardless of the number of times the test is given. Clearly, if the teacher were to give the same talk on different occasions, it would vary a lot.

2 It is possible to use the (recorded) voices of native-speakers or fluent speakers of English.

3 It is possible to play recordings of conversations involving two or more speakers – something which is far better than the teacher trying to read aloud the voices of different speakers.

Short statements and conversations

As listening to long talks in a foreign language can be very demanding on students, it is generally more appropriate for learners in the early stages to listen to fairly short statements and conversations of only two or three lines. A number of listening tests contain short statements in the form of instructions or directions. Other listening tests contain short conversations on which questions (or pictures) are based.

Simple instructions

Writing simple instructions for listening comprehension tests is usually a straightforward task. For example, you may put certain objects on a table and ask individual students to do things with them:

Put the pen next to the ruler.
Now pick up the longer of the two pencils.
Write your full name on the paper near the ruler.
Put the pencil under/behind the box of chalk.
Pick up the newspaper and open it at page 2.
Read out the headline in the second column at the top of
  page 2.

You can then ask questions about the objects:

Is the ruler made of wood or plastic?
What colour are the pencils?
How many pieces of chalk are there in the box?

This type of listening test is useful for progress testing at the elementary or intermediate levels. Unfortunately, it is difficult to test a large number of students at the same time.

Statements, questions and short conversations

These items require students to listen to statements, questions and short conversations and then to choose the correct written option from a choice of four. Examples are given here of each type of item.

1 *Statements*

Students hear:

Ann wouldn't be late so much if she knew she'd be punished.

Students read:

A Ann is often late and is punished.
B Ann is often late but is never punished.
C Ann is rarely late and is never punished.
D Ann is rarely late and thus isn't often punished.

This type of item usually tests an awareness of grammar as well as listening ability. It is of limited use in proficiency tests when a more general assessment of language ability is required.

2 *Questions*

Although this type of item is an attempt to simulate a real speech situation, it is still rather artificial. However, it is sometimes useful at the elementary and lower intermediate stages in progress and selection tests.

Students hear:

How did you do it?

Students read:

A No, I didn't.
B I'm fine, thanks.
C By loosening the screws.
D About half an hour.

---

3 *Short conversations*

Such short conversations as those shown here are often referred to as conversational exchanges. In some ways such conversational exchanges are among the most useful types of item at the lower levels.

Students hear:

Man: Can I have an appointment with Dr Lawson tomorrow?
Woman: Let me see. He usually gets here at nine in the morning and he's free for ten minutes then. Otherwise it'll have to be ten-twenty.
Man: In that case, I'll be waiting for him as soon as he arrives.

Students read:

At what time does the man want to see Dr Lawson?
   A 9.00 a.m.
   B 9.10 a.m.
   C 10 a.m.
   D 10.20 a.m.

Completing pictures

Far better for the average class are ordinary pencil-and-paper tests. You can still give instructions to the students but this time they can carry out your instructions while quietly sitting at their desks. For example, you can instruct them to complete a simple form or a picture.

Completing pictures according to certain instructions is often preferable since students are involved in drawing rather than in writing. If a student is required to write and gets the answer wrong, we have no means of knowing why that student has failed to carry out the task successfully. Is it because he or she has not understood the instructions? Or is it because he or she has understood the instructions but cannot carry out the actual writing part of the task? Provided that drawing tasks are kept simple, this problem will not arise when a student is asked to complete a picture. If a student fails to complete the picture in the required way, we will know at once that it is because the student has not understood the instructions.

The following is an example of a listening comprehension test in which students are required to complete a picture. Note the attempt to make the instructions sound as natural as possible and to provide a realistic context for them.

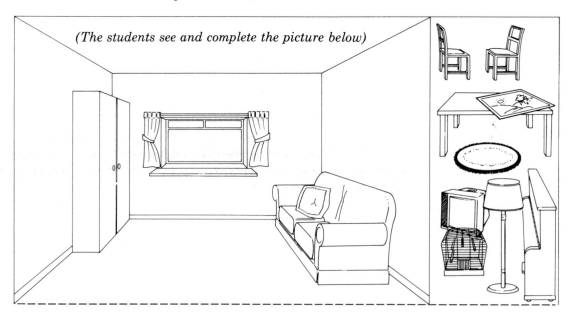

(The students see and complete the picture below)

(The students hear the following instructions)

You're moving into a new flat. Some men are helping you to move all the furniture into the lounge in your new flat. They've already put the sofa and a cupboard in the room. And there are curtains on the windows.

Listen carefully to these instructions and then draw the furniture in the room. The drawings on the box at the right of the picture will help you.

1 First put the table just in front of the window, but be careful! Don't knock the table legs against the door.

2 Next take the two chairs and put one on the left side of the table – you know, the same side as the cupboard.

3 Now where shall I put the other one? You know, it's a lovely view from the window. Let's put it in front of the table so I can look out of the window when I have a meal.

etc.

Following directions

Marking a journey on a map is similar in many ways to completing a picture. However, this kind of test will obviously involve the language of directions. Little or no actual drawing will be necessary, although it will be useful if students have pencils to follow the directions being given.

In the example on the following page, note that letters are included on the street plan. In addition to finding the place referred to, students are required to write the letters and names of the buildings mentioned. If you feel that this would be too difficult for your students, however, you can always omit this part of the test.

Note the attempt to make the directions sound as natural as possible (even though only the first part of the accompanying tapescript is given).

Look at your map and imagine that you have just come out of the station. You will hear some directions to Mandy's house.

Follow the directions on your map and put a cross where you think Mandy's house is.

You will also hear the names of five buildings you will see on the way.

Write the name of each building and the correct letter after it.

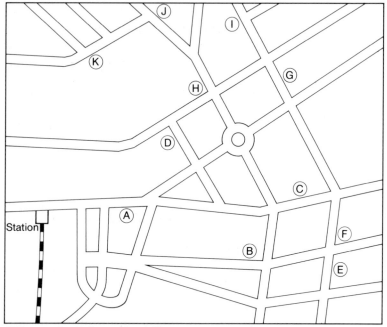

(The students hear the following directions.)

Turn right when you leave the station. Cross the road and walk straight on for about two hundred metres. On your right – that is, on the opposite side of the road – you'll see a bank: The New Eastern Bank, it's called. Just past the bank, you'll see a turning left. It isn't a right-angle or anything so sharp – more a diagonal. Turn up this road and keep straight on until the first crossroads. I'm not certain whether there are any traffic lights or not – I forget. But it's about a hundred yards before the roundabout... *etc.*

Short conversations and statements about pictures

Short conversational exchanges and statements based on pictures offer a useful way of testing listening comprehension. Students should look at the pictures while listening to each statement or conversation. Ideally, they should glance at the pictures immediately before they hear the voice on tape. Careful listening is very important as some of the items will require students to distinguish between words such as *fifty* and *fifteen*, etc. It is important for them to listen carefully until the particular conversation or series of statements has completely finished.

As drawing pictures can be very time-consuming, it is better to choose a picture which you already possess. You can use almost any poster or large picture for the purpose. Simply select your picture and write short statements about it. Make half the statements true and half false. Students then listen to each statement about the picture and write T (true) or F (false) after the number of the statement. Alternatively, you can write several short conversational exchanges (i.e. conversations consisting of only two or three lines) based on the picture and ask open-ended questions on each of the conversations.

Longer conversations and talks

Radio reports

If you can listen to any radio programmes in English, you may be able to record the following types of reports for use as listening comprehension material:

weather and traffic reports
reports on today's events
sports reports and results
news reports
advice programmes (e.g. looking after our teeth; choosing a place for a holiday)

If there are no radio programmes in English, then you might try writing your own simple reports for testing listening comprehension.

The following is an example of the type of radio report suitable for testing listening comprehension at a lower intermediate level, especially in proficiency tests. Note that only part of the report is given here.

Students read:

Listen to the travel report on the radio. You will hear about problems which people will encounter when they travel. Look at the notes and put a tick where you think there will be problems.

1 British Rail

Southern ☐   Northern ☐   Western ☐   Eastern ☐

2 Underground

Northern Line ☐   Circle Line ☐   Victoria Line ☐   Bakerloo Line ☐

3 Ferries

Dunkirk ☐   Calais ☐   Boulogne ☐   St Malo ☐

4 Flights

Britain ☐   Europe ☐   Middle East ☐   Far East ☐

Students hear:

Imagine that you are listening to the travel news on the radio. You are only interested in the problems which are mentioned. When you hear about a problem, put a tick in the right box or boxes. Do this while you are listening. At the end, the recording will be repeated.

Presenter: Good morning. It's 7.55 precisely. Here is the travel news. Mary, any problems on the railways this morning?

Mary Hill: Hello, Michael. I'm afraid today there are one or two problems. Unfortunately, there is a strike on the Southern Region and several trains have been cancelled. However, the strike doesn't seem to be spreading to the other regions and all the trains there are running as normal. Turning to the London Underground, I'm afraid that urgent repair work... *etc.*

Talks and lectures

If you give talks and short lectures for listening comprehension, remember that the test should not become a test of memory. Test students' understanding of the important points in the talk – not insignificant points which happen to be easy to test. And if you read aloud a talk instead of giving it from notes (or memory), make sure that most of the important points are repeated or re-stated in the talk. If these points are not repeated in the original written extract of the talk, re-write it so that they are repeated.

It is a good idea in some cases to give students incomplete notes and let them finish the notes as they listen to the talk. The following is given as an example of part of a talk and the accompanying notes:

Students see and complete:

Listen to the talk about dreams and fill in each blank with one word or number.

1 Dream every _____ .

2 Dream 1 ½ – _____ hrs a night.

3 Dreams _____ as night continues.

4 When lighter sleep _____ dreams... *etc.*

Students hear:

We know now that everybody dreams in approximately hourly cycles. In other words, we have a dream every hour when we are asleep. The total time we spend dreaming is between one and a half hours and two hours a night. Contrary to what many people think, our dreams last longer than a few seconds. But what is even more important, our dreams become longer as the night goes on. They start off being quite short and then gradually last longer. The first dream, for example, may last about five or ten minutes. But the last dream may last for as long as an hour. The less deeply we sleep, the longer our dreams last.

The lighter our sleep, the more we dream... *etc.*

If students have difficulty completing a line of notes or part of a table, tell them not to spend time thinking about it. They should concentrate on what is being said on the tape. If the talk is played again, they will have a second chance to complete anything they have missed.

Longer conversations

We can also buy or make recordings of fluent speakers having a conversation. It is not too difficult to write true/false statements about a conversation.

A conversation may sometimes sound more natural and interesting than a talk, especially when the people taking part in the conversation have different attitudes to a particular topic. In any case, it is useful to vary the material in a listening comprehension test, including both talks and conversations.

Testing listening with other skills

As we shall see in the next chapter, almost all the speaking tests now in use are combined with listening. In order to hold any conversation, it is necessary to listen before speaking. We listen to the person with whom we are having a conversation, constantly adapting our replies as the conversation progresses. Listening is such an integral part of speaking in everyday life that we often refer to oral interview tests as *listen-speak* tests.

Multi-mode tests

In addition, however, there are several other types of *multi-mode* tests involving listening.

> A multi-mode test is a test which contains a task (or a number of tasks) requiring the use of more than one language skill for its satisfactory completion.

Remember that multi-mode listening tests should take the form of real tasks. Such tests are primarily performance-referenced tests. The following is an example of such a multi-mode test:

> First students *listen* to a recording of newspaper boys shouting out such headlines as
>
> *Fire damage to Town Hall. Read all about it!*
> *West Germany supporters attack referee. Read all about it!*
> *Prince Charles to visit Chile. Read all about it!*
>
> The students then *discuss* what these headlines are about. After this, they *listen* to the news which is given on the radio later. Finally, they *write* a short article on one of the news items for their local newspaper.

Listening can be combined with writing in several other ways in our tests. For example, we may instruct students to answer the telephone and write down the message they hear. Students on study skills courses may be required to listen to short lectures in English and to take notes. Such ways of combining listening with writing can be used to simulate some common tasks which are very relevant to the students' needs.

Take care to avoid giving traditional kinds of listening comprehension tests which require students to answer questions orally on what they have just heard or to give an oral paraphrase. For example, a test in which students listen to a short narrative and then re-tell the story lacks any real purpose and is usually inferior to a test which measures listening on its own. If students do badly on such a test, we cannot be sure whether their poor performance arises because they have not understood the story or because they have understood it but are unable to re-tell the story.

Finally, remember that the listening skills can best be developed if they are usually taught and tested on their own as skills not dependent on other language skills.

Activities

1

Classify each of the items on page 56 according to whether it is testing a) sound differences, b) word stress, c) sentence stress, or d) intonation. How useful do you think each item is for inclusion in a progress test in the first year of learning English?

1 Listen carefully to each sentence and then finish it in any way you think is most suitable.
(The sentence is read out by the teacher or examiner, and the word or syllable in capital letters carries the main stress.)
  i) I like cycling in the COUN-try but not .....
  ii) I like CYCling in the country – not .....
  iii) I've seen a RED car but I haven't .....
  iv) We ordered FRIED rice – not ..... *etc.*

2 One sentence in each group is different from the other two sentences. Write the letter of the sentence which is different.
  i) A There was a shock for Dave when he opened the parcel.
    B There was a shock for Dave when he opened the parcel.
    C There was a sock for Dave when he opened the parcel.
  ii) A Look at that bend in the road.
    B Look at that band in the road.
    C Look at that bend in the road... *etc.*

3 If we say the same sentence in a different way, it can have a different meaning. Listen to the way the following sentences are spoken. Then choose the appropriate description.
  i) Mr and Mrs Shaw have just arrived.
    A This is an expression of surprise.
    B This is a question.
  ii) You're sure you can do it.
    A This is a straightforward statement.
    B This is an expression of surprise... *etc.*

4 Write S if the words in each pair of words are the same and D if they are different.
  i) ice   eyes   iii) joke   joke
  ii) sail   sail   iv) glass   grass... *etc.*

5 Listen carefully and underline the syllable which is stressed in each word.
  i) ad-vice   iii) in-spec-tor
  ii) fash-ion   iv) ex-plo-ra-tion... *etc.*

2

Look again at the five exercises in the section on dictation. Choose a short passage for dictation and write an appropriate exercise or item similar to one of the five exercises.

3

Comment on the following test of listening comprehension. Try to improve the test, re-writing the text and the exercise where you think it is necessary.

Listen to the short talk. Fill in the blanks in the summary after you have heard the talk.

(Spoken)

I looked up and saw several clouds floating by like huge white ships sailing on a deep blue sea. There were a few birds which were perched on the cliffs above me. Some of the birds began to spread out their wings and glide gracefully on the currents of air. In front of me there was a stream which flowed very quietly under a small bridge near me. It hardly made a sound. In the distance I could see some waves rolling gently on the beach. There was someone standing there all alone. Then I suddenly noticed something else. It was a rowing-boat and it was drifting out to sea. There was someone inside it!

(Written)

What did the speaker actually say? Write the correct word in each blank.

The speaker looked up and saw several clouds _____ by

like huge white ships. Some birds were _____ on

the cliffs above him. They _____ out their wings and

_____ gracefully through the air. A stream

_____ quietly near the speaker and in the distance

he could see some waves _____ gently on the beach.

Then he suddenly _____ a rowing-boat drifting out to sea.

4

Look again at the examples on Page 48 ('Completing pictures') and on Page 49 ('Following directions'). Finish each test by writing more instructions and directions.

Discussion

1 How often should dictation tests and exercises be given to your class? Discuss.

2 Try to look at the transcript of any listening comprehension test which you have heard or used. In what ways is it similar or different from a written text?

3 Discuss with a colleague any listening comprehension test which requires students to complete a picture. In what ways can it be improved?

4 Discuss how you would select a suitable radio talk for use as a listening comprehension test. The talk should last no longer than five minutes.

Testing speaking skills

Pronunciation

Pronouncing words in isolation

The importance of the listening skills in almost all tests of speaking should never be underestimated. It is impossible for students to pronounce a word correctly unless they first hear and recognise the precise sound of that word.

When we learn a foreign language, we often hear sounds which are completely new and unfamiliar to us. For example, if we have never come across the *th* sound [θ] in English, the natural tendency is for us to substitute a familiar sound from our own language (generally either *t* [t] or *sh* [ʃ] for the unfamiliar sound *th* [θ]).

Although we may not distinguish between certain sounds in our own language, this difference in English may be crucial. For example, there is no difference in Spanish between the vowel sound in *ship* [i] and that in *sheep* [iː] or in Arabic between the first consonant sound in *pull* [p] and that in *bull* [b].

In the early stages of learning English, therefore, it is useful to base our pronunciation tests on minimal pairs: that is, pairs of words which differ only in one sound:

bud	bird	ferry	fairy
nip	nib	boss	bus
pill	pail	knit	lit
ball	bowl	fry	fly
sheet	seat	support	sport
etc.			

In the early stages of learning English, students can be shown pictures and asked to identify the object in each picture. Each picture is based on a possible source of confusion. For example

Picture 1 tests the student's ability to distinguish between *pen* and *pan*, Picture 2 between *ship* and *sheep*, Picture 3 between *bird* and *bud*, Picture 4 between *van* and *fan*.

Pronouncing words in sentences

Later you can ask students to read aloud sentences containing the problem sounds which you want to test. Sentences are, of course, preferable because they provide a context for the sounds (as in real life). They help to discourage students unnaturally exaggerating a certain sound when they pronounce it in an oral test.

There were several people standing in the hole.	*(hole/hall)*
Are you going to sail your boat today?	*(sail/sell)*
Do you like this sport?	*(sport/spot)*

Reading aloud

Reading aloud can offer a useful way of testing pronunciation provided that you give a student a few minutes to look at the reading text first. When you choose suitable texts to read aloud, it is useful to imagine actual situations when someone may read something aloud. Ask yourself what someone may actually want to read aloud in real life. Sometimes, for example, people read aloud letters or instructions.

The following example consists of simple instructions on how to use a public telephone. The student would be given a copy of the instructions only, but the examiner's copy might appear as follows:

Text	Examiner's notes
First pick up the <u>handset</u>	fɜːst; stress on hænd
and listen <u>for</u> the dialling <u>tone</u>.	fə (weak form); təʊn
Then put in a <u>fifty</u> cent <u>coin</u>.	fɪfti; main stress
Now <u>dial</u> the number you require	daɪəl
and listen <u>for</u> a ringing tone.	linking 'r'
If you hear an <u>engaged tone</u>,	ɪnˈgeɪdʒd; falling intonation
<u>replace</u> the handset and <u>try</u>	rɪˈpleɪs (not /z/)
again later.	
Your coin will be <u>returned</u>	final consonant
automatically.	

Re-telling stories

A test which is more useful in certain ways than reading aloud is the re-telling of a story or incident. If you use this kind of test, give the student a story to read silently first. Then ask the student to tell the story he or she has just read. If the story has been carefully chosen, the student will use those elements of pronunciation which you wish to test. Remember that the sole purpose of such a test is pronunciation and do not deduct marks for any incorrect reporting or inaccurate oral summaries.

Using pictures

Pictures are very useful for testing the speaking skills. First, choose the picture(s) very carefully as a picture often influences the language forms which the students use. Secondly, make sure that students can see the pictures for a few minutes before they have to describe them. Thirdly, remember that oral work based on pictures is often best assessed as part of a lesson rather than as part of a test. When included in a test, oral assessment can be very time-consuming.

Pictures for description

Single pictures, photographs and posters can be used for simple descriptions from students. When preparing for a test, give students plenty of practice describing pictures of objects, people and scenes. In some pictures students will be required to use their imagination and say what they think has just happened or is about to happen.

Describing pictures is also an activity which you can give students fairly regularly. Ask students to talk about a picture in groups, describing the people, objects and places in the picture, saying what the people are doing and where the various objects are. Don't ask too many questions about a picture but provide as much stimulus and help as necessary. Encourage students to use their imagination. Ask them to try to guess what has just happened in the picture or what is about to happen. Ask them to give reasons to justify their answers to these questions.

Pictures for comparison

A more interesting test is one which involves the description of two fairly similar pictures. Two students are each given a picture and instructed to talk about it. The purpose of this activity is to find out in what ways the two pictures are different – without either student actually seeing both pictures. Genuine conversation is thus encouraged in addition to the more formal descriptions of the pictures. Students, for example, ask each other questions, contradict, agree and in general use language to achieve a particular task.

Several newspapers and puzzle books contain pictures which are similar to each other in most respects but which require readers to spot minute differences. Unfortunately, such differences are usually so small that it is almost impossible for two people to find these differences without looking very carefully at *both* pictures. Consequently, such pictures are not as useful for this type of speaking test as might at first seem to be the case.

Fortunately, there are now plenty of picture composition books for teaching English as a foreign language. Books such as *Composition through Pictures, Beginning Composition through Pictures* and *Writing through Pictures* (J. B. Heaton, Longman) are only a few of the many books which contain a variety of pictures useful for all types of speaking tests.

The following two pictures, for example, have been taken from
Beginning Composition through Pictures and can be used
effectively for purposes of comparison in the type of speaking test
described in the previous paragraph.

Sequences of pictures

A sequence of pictures telling a story can also be used to test speaking ability. Students should be instructed to tell a story (using the past tense forms) rather than simply describe what is happening in each picture.

A sequence of pictures showing a process may be used in the same way. The following example of a simple process (changing a wheel after a puncture) has been taken from *Writing 2* (R. A. Knight, Cassell).

fix the jack
in position

lower

tighten

raise

a flat tyre

put it in the boot

loosen the nuts

do up

put on

take off

Speaking tests in which a story is told or a process is described involve individual students rather than pairs of students. If you want to use an activity which results in two students not only describing pictures but also talking to each other, you can take a sequence of pictures telling a story (or describing a process) and mix up the order of the pictures. Give half the pictures to one student and half to another. Two students are then required to talk about their pictures and then decide on the correct sequence of pictures. When they have finished, they should lay out all the pictures in front of them and discuss their attempt.

Pictures with speech bubbles

Another use of pictures for testing speaking requires students to guess what the people in the pictures are saying. Comics, picture stories and cartoons can be used in this particular way if they contain pictures with speech bubbles. Simply delete the words in the speech bubbles and ask students to guess what the characters are saying. This can be done either individually or in pairs. However, remember that we are not interested primarily in whether students guess correctly or not. Our sole concern is the language they use for this purpose. If students have difficulty guessing what someone might be saying, be ready to prompt them. Your aim should always be to get the students talking as much as possible.

Maps

Maps can be used for testing students' ability to give directions. If students are tested in pairs, one student can be required to give directions while the other follows these directions and traces the route on his or her map.

Oral interviews

In real life the two skills of listening and speaking are fully integrated in most everyday situations involving communication. Consequently, an excellent way of testing speaking is the oral interview since listening and speaking can be assessed in a natural situation.

When the speaking test forms part of an achievement or

proficiency test, it is useful to start by asking students to give personal details: their names, addresses, hobbies, likes, dislikes, etc. This part of the test is designed partly to obtain important information from the students being interviewed and partly to put them at ease. During such conversations, a student may be asked to spell a word (e.g. his or her name, the name of the street where he or she lives, etc.) or read out a number (e.g. his or her candidate's number, telephone number, postal code, etc.).

Asking questions

Care should be taken to prevent the interview from becoming an interrogation. The following questions asked in rapid succession may result in an unfair and unpleasant interview, resembling an interrogation more than an educational test:

When do you get up every morning?
What do you have for breakfast?
How do you travel to school?

It is, of course, important to draw up a list of suitable questions which you can ask students. You can then choose the most appropriate questions from the list for a certain student or a particular interview. Try to ask questions which may lead to interesting answers, but always be ready to respond to any answer with your own comments and observations. Talk as naturally as you can in English. Don't worry unduly about your own standard of English; a real speaking test is concerned with communication.

Try to soften some of your questions. For example, instead of asking straightforward questions in quick succession, make statements and ask questions more subtly:

I've often wondered where Plum Tree Road is.
I usually take sandwiches to school for lunch – I suppose you do, too?
They say that your college has a very good basketball team.

It is all too easy for you to adopt the natural position of a superior talking to an inferior when you test students. Consequently, you should try hard to establish a friendly relationship. Contribute to the conversation, telling the student about your own likes, dislikes, habits, etc. At the same time, you should take care to avoid doing too much talking. It is not unusual for an interviewer to talk more than a student and then award a high mark. Such interviewers are, in fact, assessing their own performance!

Marking

Although marking speaking tests will be treated at some length later in this chapter, it is appropriate to state an important principle here; namely, never mark in front of a student. Nothing is more discouraging for a student than to enter into conversation with someone who is constantly breaking off to enter marks and comments. The student should be constantly reassured that *what* he or she says is being treated as important – rather than *how* he or she says it. If possible, wait until the student has left the room before you enter your marks and comments.

In spite of all your attempts, it may sometimes be impossible to avoid tension and nervousness on the part of many students. Such feelings of tension can affect their performance and change the way they behave in an interview. For example, students at a certain age sometimes become unnaturally quiet or aggressive.

Testing students in pairs

One way of making the interview less tense is to test two students at the same time. This method has the advantage of enabling you to hear the students talking to someone in their own peer group – equal to equal rather than inferior to superior. Moreover, if you give them a task to perform, they will be able to demonstrate their ability to use language naturally for a real purpose. For example, the two students might be asked to find out the differences between two similar pictures or to re-arrange pictures to tell a story. Or you may ask the students before the interview to prepare a short quiz to give to each other.

Even though you can test two students in only a slightly longer time than it takes to test one student, testing the speaking skills remains very time-consuming. However, there are other more efficient methods of assessing speaking ability and these are discussed in Chapter 7 'Continuous Assessment'.

Grading oral ability

A major difficulty in testing speaking is the actual method used of awarding marks. Whatever system is adopted, the marking itself is very subjective. We must take care, for example, to avoid allowing a student's personality to influence the grade we award – if we are concerned with language ability and achievement in a progress or placement test.

Grammatical accuracy

One problem relates to grammatical accuracy and general fluency. For example, how would you mark a student who has succeeded in communicating what he or she wants to express but who has made a lot of grammatical errors? Would that student score more or fewer marks than another student who has made no grammatical errors at all but who has said nothing relevant or appropriate to the conversation?

Example 1

Examiner: You're very late for the interview.
   Student: Yes, I'm being sorry for my late arriving to interview. My mother is being very ill in the hospital with the rheumatism.

Example 2

Examiner: You're very late for the interview.
   Student: Yes, thank you. My name's Javier Hernandez and I'm a student at the New Oxford Institute. I like talking in English very much.

When a student makes a grammatical error in the spoken language, first ask yourself if the error causes a breakdown in communication. Do you have difficulty in understanding what the student is saying? If so, you should penalise the student when you award the mark. If the mistake does not really interfere with what is being communicated, then it is advisable to ignore it. In Example 1 above, we can understand the student without much difficulty at all and thus we may ignore the mistakes. Remember, however, there may be times when you wish to avoid giving the impression to students that anything they say is perfectly acceptable.

Using a rating scale

You are strongly advised to use a scale for grading students' performances on speaking tests rather than a marking scheme. Marks mean nothing in themselves: for example, seventy per cent can be a high mark if a test is very difficult or a low mark if it is easy. Marks also mean different things to different teachers. Few teachers would agree on the same mark if they were assessing a student's oral ability in an interview. Even if you were to try to devise an analytical marking scheme (e.g. five marks for grammar with half a mark being deducted for each error, five marks for pronunciation, five for relevance, etc.), the marks would vary greatly from one examiner to another.

Consequently, it is much better to use a rating scale containing short descriptions of each grade in the scale. When we grade a student's speaking ability, we simply read through the scale and choose the most appropriate description for the particular student. Many international exams use such scales and include them in their sample booklets. However, instead of copying a particular scale, it is much better to produce your own scale. Such a scale will be far more suitable for your own students and purposes.

Start by describing in one or two sentences what an average successful student should be able to do. Write briefly about his or her performance. Remember, however, that it is important to be realistic. You would not, for example, expect a student to speak with native-speaker fluency after only two years of learning English for a few hours a week.

The following is a description of the performance of an average student at the lower intermediate level at the end of a particular course. The student is judged to have been reasonably successful on the course. If we work on a six point scale, therefore, we would expect this student to be at level 4.

Pronunciation is still influenced a little by the first language. The student can be expected to make a few grammatical errors, only one or two of which will cause serious confusion. The student still searches for words when he or she speaks, but the general meaning of the message is quite clear even though there are a few unnatural pauses. The student will convey the general meaning fairly clearly, although a few interruptions are usually necessary. However, the student's intention is always clear, and the student will have mastered most of the speaking skills practised on the course.

We would next write a description of level 3 – the level reached by a student who is only slightly below average in his or her achievement.

> Pronunciation will be influenced to a large extent by the first language. The student can be expected to make several pronunciation and grammatical errors, some of which may be serious and cause considerable confusion ...

We would then go on to a similar brief description of level 5 – the level reached by a student who is very good in his or her achievement.

> Pronunciation will be only slightly influenced by the first language. Although the student can be expected to make a few grammatical errors, most of the sentences produced will be correct ...

Next we would describe level 2 – the level of a student who has not achieved a satisfactory performance. Finally, we would describe level 6 – the performance level of a very successful student and level 1 – the performance level of an extremely poor student.

When put into note form, the rating scale might appear as follows.

> **6** Pronunciation good – only 2 or 3 grammatical errors – not much searching for words – very few long pauses – fairly easy to understand – very few interruptions necessary – has mastered all oral skills on course

> **5** Pronunciation slightly influenced by L1 – a few grammatical errors but most sentences correct – sometimes searches for words – not too many long pauses – general meaning fairly clear but a few interruptions necessary – has mastered almost all oral skills on course

> **4** Pronunciation influenced a little by L1 – a few grammatical errors but only 1 or 2 causing serious confusion – searches for words – a few unnatural pauses – conveys general meaning fairly clearly – a few interruptions usually necessary but intention always clear – has mastered most of oral skills on course

----

3 Pronunciation influenced by L1 – pronunciation and grammatical errors – several errors cause serious confusion – longer pauses to search for word or meaning – fairly limited expression – much can be understood although some effort needed for parts – some interruptions necessary – has mastered only some of oral skills on course

2 Several serious pronunciation errors – basic grammar errors – unnaturally long pauses – very limited expression – needs some effort to understand much of it – interruptions often necessary and sometimes has difficulty in explaining or making meaning clearer – only a few of oral skills on course mastered

1 A lot of serious pronunciation errors – many basic grammar errors – full of unnaturally long pauses – very halting delivery – extremely limited expression – almost impossible to understand – interruptions constantly necessary but cannot explain or make meaning clearer – very few of oral skills on course mastered

Note that a six-point scale is used in order to avoid a middle level. If, for example, a five-point scale were used, there would be a tendency for many teachers to place a lot of students at level 3 – the middle level. A six-point scale compels us to decide whether a certain student is slightly above average (level 4) or slightly below average (level 3), thus enabling us to divide the middle range of students into 2 levels.

Finally, note that level 3 (slightly below average) should not necessarily indicate a fail grade if the test is used as an achievement test. We would generally wish to set our fail/unsatisfactory level at level 1 or 2, leaving level 3 and above to indicate pass grades.

Using a language laboratory

The chief drawback of oral interview tests is the time which is needed. Each student must be tested individually, and even a short test which takes only five or ten minutes becomes very time-consuming when given separately to thirty students.

The use of a language laboratory makes it possible to give oral tests to a large number of students in a short time. It would be foolish to claim that a speaking test using pre-recorded material can ever be superior to a genuine face-to-face oral interview. Nevertheless, for certain limited purposes, a language laboratory can offer a means of encouraging students to speak English and to become accustomed to responding to various questions which may possibly arise in real life.

Examples will be given in this section of the types of oral exercises and activities suitable for use in the language laboratory.

Questions about likes, dislikes, etc.

Questions are recorded on tape and pauses left on the tape for students to record their replies.

---

1 What's your hobby?
   (PAUSE) . . . .

2 Why do you find it interesting?
   (PAUSE) . . . .

3 What advice would you give to someone about to take up this hobby?
   (PAUSE) . . . .
   etc.

Although this type of test attempts to simulate a real life situation, it is of little real use. There is still something unnatural about a student talking to a machine. At best, the student is replying to questions which come from a disembodied voice. The test itself is much harder than it would have been had the student been able to see the person who is talking. Consider how much harder it is to speak to someone in a foreign language over the telephone than it is face to face.

Questions and statements in social situations

This type of question tests students' abilities to make fairly conventional responses to questions and statements. Students must show their ability to express agreement, disagreement, complaints, apologies, etc.

1 Do you mind if I open this window?
(PAUSE) . . . .

2 Do you have the time?
(PAUSE) . . . .

3 I'm sorry I'm rather late.
(PAUSE) . . . .
etc.

Mini situations

In this type of test students are given a real-life situation, usually recorded on tape (although sometimes given in printed form). They are asked to respond appropriately to each situation.

1 You meet a friend of yours who has just come out of hospital. What do you say?

2 The telephone rings and someone asks to speak to Mr Len Shaw. You've never heard of him. What do you say?

3 Someone asks you to see a film with him, but you'd rather see it with your best friend. What do you say?
etc.

Conversations (1)

The following question type is based on certain everyday situations: introducing oneself to a friend, asking for information, giving directions, making an appointment to see a doctor/dentist, booking a hotel room, a table in a restaurant, etc., choosing something to buy, making or replying to requests for help, etc. A brief explanation of the situation is given before the conversation starts. Students can reply to questions and even ask questions. Remember, however, that there is no script and students can only respond to what they hear on the tape.

Can you tell me the way to the nearest post office?
(PAUSE) . . . .
Thanks. Do you know what time it closes?
(PAUSE) . . . .

> Thanks a lot. You've been very helpful. I wonder how much it'll cost to send a letter to Britain.
> (PAUSE) ....
> It's expensive sending letters abroad these days, isn't it?
> (PAUSE) ....

This kind of conversation is sometimes called a dialogue of the deaf since the recorded voice continues in the same predetermined way no matter what is said by the student. Look how absurd this version of the preceding conversation is!

A: Can you tell me the way to the nearest post office?
B: Sorry, I'm a stranger here.
A: Thanks. Do you know what time it closes?
B: I've got absolutely no idea at all.
A: Thanks a lot. You've been very helpful. I wonder how much it'll cost to send a letter to Britain.
B: Sorry, I'm in a hurry. I can't waste my time talking to you.
A: It's expensive sending letters abroad these days, isn't it?
B: Please shut up and go away.

Conversations (2)

The following type of test overcomes the weakness referred to above because prompts are whispered, indicating how students should respond (in general terms). In this sense, it may not be quite as natural as the conversation previously described, but it can often work better as a stimulus for controlled conversation.

Students hear:

You want to buy a cassette radio in a small shop.

Shopkeeper:	Good morning. Can I help you?
Whispered prompt:	*You want to buy a cassette radio.*
	(PAUSE) ....
Shopkeeper:	Certainly. This one in the window is one of the latest models – and the most reasonable in price.
Prompt:	*Ask the price.*
	(PAUSE) ....

```
    Shopkeeper:  It's £42. That's excellent value for money
                 because a similar cassette recorder
                 would cost over £60.
        Prompt:  Enquire if he has any other models.
                 (PAUSE) . . . . . . . . . . . . . . . . . . . . . . . . . . . . .
    Shopkeeper:  Yes, there's this on the top shelf, but it's
                 more expensive. It also comes with a
                 case.
        Prompt:  You want to look at it.
                 (PAUSE) . . . . . . . . . . . . . . . . . . . . . . . . . . . . .
                 etc.
```

Conversations (3)

In the following item the student is asked to take part in a short conversation after having read a diary extract containing a week's appointments.

Students read:

MONDAY	8.00 p.m.	Disco
TUESDAY	3.00 p.m.	See doctor
	6.00 p.m.	Go to library
WEDNESDAY	1.00 p.m.	Choir rehearsal
	7.30 p.m.	Concert – Shenton Choir

Students hear:

Today is Sunday. Your friend Don phones you. Talk to him.

Don: Hello. It's Don here.
(PAUSE) . . . .

Don: Are you going to the disco tomorrow evening?
(PAUSE) . . . .

Don: Are you doing anything on Tuesday evening? I was wondering about playing tennis.
(PAUSE) . . . .

Don: By the way, you haven't forgotten about meeting Ann and me for lunch at quarter to one on Wednesday, have you?
(PAUSE) . . . .
etc.

Testing speaking with other skills

We saw in the previous chapter that listening and speaking are often inseparable, especially in tests containing conversations and interviews.

Speaking can also be tested in relation to reading. A useful test may contain a written text for students to read and discuss. The students will talk about the text, discussing it with their friends or with the examiner. In tests concerned with study skills, students may be required to read an article or a report so that they can discuss it in a group.

Remember that multi-mode tests (see page 54) should be task-based tests and should measure students' ability to perform the kinds of tasks which might later confront them in everyday life.

Activities

1
Select a picture story which comprises at least six pictures. Cut the pictures up and jumble them, giving one half of the pictures to one student and the other half to another student. Instruct the two students to try to find the correct order in which the pictures should be placed. Each student should talk about his or her own pictures and listen to the other student doing the same. The two students should show each other their pictures only when they have decided on the correct order.

2
Write twenty suitable questions for use in an oral interview with your students. Your questions should relate to their situation, their age group, their habits and interests. Remember to try to soften or disguise some of your questions so that the interview does not become an interrogation. Think about the students' possible answers and about the comments and replies which you might make so as to contribute to the conversation.

3
Describe in one or two sentences the situation in which each of the following utterances might be spoken. Then write test

questions similar to those shown in 'Mini situations' on Page 73.

---

1 Did you manage to relax and was it a nice change?
2 I'm extremely sorry. Can I possibly pay for it?
3 Could you explain how you get £125? I make it £95.
4 I would if I could but I've already arranged to see Tim at six.
5 Don't worry. I'm certain we'll be on time.
6 Let's make a dash for it to the nearest tree or shelter.

4

Write appropriate prompts to help the student participate in the following conversation. Your prompts should be similar to those in 'Conversations (2)' on Page 74.

Voice:	Are you going to watch TV tonight? There's a very good programme on Hong Kong.
Student:	....
Voice:	I think it's seven thirty to eight thirty.
Student:	....
Voice:	It's on Channel 4. It should be very interesting. I was in Hong Kong for a week last year, you know.
Student:	....
Voice:	Sorry. I said I went to Hong Kong last year. I stayed there for a week.
Student:	....
Voice:	At the Heung Wing Court.
Student:	....
Voice:	H-E-U-N-G W-I-N-G – Heung Wing.
Student:	....
Voice:	It was about $1,200 dollars a night, but it was worth it. It's a top-class hotel.

Discussion

1 Describe briefly the types of pictures which you find most useful for encouraging oral work with your students.

2 Working with a colleague or group of colleagues, select a sequence of pictures and then re-arrange them in any order. Give half the pictures to one student and the other half to another student. Record their discussion when they are trying to put the pictures in the correct order. How does their speech differ from the speech they use normally in answering your questions? Discuss.

3 Discuss with a colleague your reasons for choosing six topics on which to ask questions in an oral interview test.

4 Discuss any tape which you have used for oral work. How far does it enable students to practise speaking?

Testing reading skills

Vocabulary

Tests of vocabulary often provide a good guide to reading ability. It is usually necessary for students to demonstrate not only a knowledge of the meaning of a particular word but also an awareness of the other words with which it is generally used (i.e. collocation). However, in addition to their usefulness in proficiency tests, vocabulary tests are also useful in progress tests as they lend themselves to follow-up work in class.

It is important at the outset to decide which words you expect your students to recognise (i.e. their *passive* or *receptive* vocabulary) and which words you expect them to use (i.e. their *active* or *productive* vocabulary). Remember that most people can recognise far more words than they can actually use.

Multiple-choice items

Multiple-choice items are often useful for testing vocabulary. In the following example, the words listed under the sentence (A, B, C and D) are called options: *film* (B) is called the correct option or the answer while *screen* (A), *showing* (C) and *acting* (D) are called distractors:

There's a good _____ at the Odeon tonight.
  A screen B film C showing D acting

Writing multiple-choice items is not too difficult after you have had a little practice. If you find it takes you too long to write four options, write only three options in your progress tests. For most classroom purposes, three options are enough. Remember that your distractors should appear correct to any students who are not sure of the answer. Avoid writing absurd distractors which everyone can easily see are wrong. On the other hand, however, all the distractors should be written within the students' range of proficiency and at the same level as the correct option.

Always make sure that each multiple-choice item has only one correct answer. It is sometimes very easy to write two options which could be correct. In the following item, both answers B and D are correct.

We went to Jimmy's Restaurant last night and had an excellent _____ there.

   A plate B meal C cook D dish

Finally, remember the importance of context. The multiple-choice vocabulary test in Activity 1 at the end of this chapter provides an example of a vocabulary test in the context of a conversation. Note that it is also possible to test vocabulary by underlining a key word in a sentence and then providing four options:

I can't <u>bear</u> people who shout a lot.

   A support B tolerate C admire D resist

Matching items

Matching items are also very useful for testing vocabulary in context. Instruct students to write the correct word from the story at the side of each word listed below it.

Dave Shaw was very keen to succeed in his first big game in the senior football league. During the first forty minutes he played with great skill, scoring one goal and helping one of his team mates to score another goal.

After the second goal, however, he discovered that he had made a dreadful mistake. He was playing for the wrong side!

The mix-up began ...
etc.

Write the most suitable word from the passage at the side of each of the following words. (Both words should have the same meaning in the passage.) The first two have been done for you.

match	_ *game*
terrible	_ **dreadful**
ability	_____
eager	_____
team	_____
confusion	_____

Completion items

The two item types treated previously in this section test the
recognition of words and word meanings. The following type of
item tests a student's ability to produce appropriate words:
production. It consists of a conversation containing blanks in
place of the words being tested.

'Are you a newspaper _____?'
'Yes, I work for the *Morning Sun*.'

'There's a very good story in today's paper about someone
who made a fortune cleaning windows.'

'Was that the story in the paper with the _____
"Ladder to Success"?'

Writing items containing blanks sometimes gives rise to certain
problems. For example, although the word *headline* is clearly the
word which is required in the last item above, it is quite possible
for a student to write *title* and obtain full marks. Giving the first
letter of the missing word can overcome this problem.

Reading tests: multiple-choice items

Multiple-choice items offer a good way of testing students'
reading comprehension. However, it is usually extremely difficult
to write four good options (one correct answer and three
incorrect answers) for each multiple-choice item on a reading
passage because frequently insufficient information is provided in
the passage. As a result, you are strongly advised to limit each
multiple-choice item you write to three options, especially for
classroom progress test.

Re-writing part of the paragraph

Sometimes it may be necessary for you to re-write part of the
passage or add to it in order to include information for another
distractor. For example, in the following multiple-choice item,
option C is clearly wrong as it does not relate to anything at all
in the reading passage.

> As I gazed at the peaceful scene, I suddenly noticed a yacht gliding slowly across the bay. It looked almost like a big ship.
>
> What did the writer see as he looked in front of him?
> A A big ship.
> B A yacht.
> CA helicopter.

Even if we omit C, it seems impossible to write a distractor which is reasonable. We simply cannot get more than two distractors for this item, given the limited amount of information available. Consequently, it is necessary for us to go back to this part of the reading passage and add information which will allow us to write a plausible distractor:

> As I gazed at the peaceful scene, I suddenly noticed a yacht gliding slowly across the bay. It looked almost like a big ship. Overhead the sky was clear. There was no sign of the helicopter which had circled above me the day before.

Avoiding matching words

Try to avoid items which only require students to match words in the text. In the next example students can easily choose the correct answer even if they cannot really understand what is happening in the story.

> Henry was looking for his cat when he suddenly saw a large black dog several hundred metres in front of him.
>
> When Henry was in the park, he suddenly saw _____ .
> A   his cat
> B   a large black dog
> C   nothing at all

We can easily re-write part of the reading passage to prevent a student from obtaining the correct answer simply by matching words and phrases.

> Henry was looking for his cat in the park when a large black animal suddenly appeared several hundred metres in front of him. At first he thought it was a newly-born pony. It ran up, wagged its tail and lay down at his feet. When he got up to go, it followed him and wouldn't go away. It had a collar round its neck but there was no name on the collar.

Writing grammatically correct options

It is important to make all the options grammatically correct if you use incomplete sentences in a multiple-choice item.

> Her favourite sports were _____.
> A   swimming and playing hockey
> B   volleyball
> C   cycling and tennis

The second option in the item above, for example, would be grammatically unacceptable when combined with the incomplete sentence: i.e. *Her favourite sports were volleyball.* Thus, clever students would avoid this answer simply because they would know it is grammatically incorrect rather than because they have understood the reading passage.

Writing options of equal length

Make all your options equal in length in the same multiple-choice item. Some teachers tend to make the correct answer longer than the others – usually because they want to make sure that it is absolutely correct. Clever students can often spot correct answers in this way. Although you haven't even seen the reading passage on which the following item is based, which option do you think will probably be correct?

> Why did Tina fall asleep during the film?
> A   She was very tired.
> B   She was not very interested in most of the film as she had seen it before.
> C   She had taken some medicine.

Mixing item types

Finally, do not try too hard to write a lot of multiple-choice items on one reading passage. Some passages will simply not allow for several multiple-choice items. If you find yourself spending a lot of time trying to write options for multiple-choice items, use one or two open-ended questions instead of multiple-choice items. Open-ended questions are those questions which require answers in a student's own words.

Reading tests: true/false items

True/false items offer a very reliable way of testing a student's reading comprehension provided that there are enough such items in a reading test. You will find it much easier and quicker, moreover, to write true/false items than multiple-choice items. Unlike multiple-choice items, a large number of true/false items can be written on a fairly short reading text. Hence true/false items are more suitable for classroom progress and achievement tests.

Many teachers argue that true/false items encourage students to guess, but there has so far been no real evidence that this is true. Students guess only when a test is so difficult that they have simply no idea what an answer should be. In almost every other case, students will use the knowledge and skills they have in order to decide on a correct answer.

Try to write each true/false statement as clearly and as briefly as you can. Use simple English and try to write your sentences at a lower level of difficulty than the reading text. In this way, the comprehension problems which you are testing will lie in the passage itself and not in the questions which follow.

Include in the instructions the number of statements which are true and of those which are false. For example, the following instruction will prove very helpful to students in letting them know precisely what you expect them to do:
Six of the following statements are true and six are false. Write T after each true statement and F after each false statement.

Here is an example showing part of a true/false reading test item. You will note that it is in the form of a newspaper report.

An eight-month old hippopotamus named Susan began a
journey by lorry and plane yesterday from the National Zoo
in Washington to Singapore. Zoo-keepers hope that she will
be a companion for a lonely male hippopotamus, reports say.
Singapore Zoo has spent a long time looking for a new mate
for their hippo, named Congo. Ever since the death of Lucy,
his mate, Congo has been sad and lonely, a spokesman said.
etc.

1 Susan was a gift from Washington National
   Zoo to Singapore Zoo.   _____

2 Congo, a male hippopotamus in Washington
   Zoo, was sad and lonely because Susan had
   left for Singapore.   _____

3 Susan was just over one year old when she
   left the National Zoo in Washington.   _____
etc.

Sometimes questions may be used instead of statements in this
type of item. Students simply indicate whether the answer is *yes*
or *no*. Note that in the following example, the second true/false
statement above has been changed into two questions for the sake
of simplicity and clarity.

1 Was Susan a gift from Washington National
   Zoo to Singapore Zoo?   _____

2 Was Congo a male hippopotamus in
   Washington National Zoo?   _____

3 Was he sad and lonely because Susan had
   left him to go to another zoo?   _____

4 Was Susan just over one year old when she
   left the National Zoo in Washington?   _____
etc.

If you write true/false statements rather than yes/no questions,
you can develop this type of item by providing a third option: *not
stated/information not given*. However, this option is recommended
only for the intermediate levels and above as it makes the test

more difficult. In addition, it reduces the element of guessing since there are three options (true/false/not stated) rather than two options (true/false).

The following example includes a suitable instruction and shows how this modified type of item works. The statements have been based on the newspaper report given earlier.

Some of the following statements are true and others are false. Write T after each true statement and F after each false statement. If the information is not given in the newspaper report, put a question mark (?).

1 Susan was a gift from Washington National Zoo to Singapore Zoo.
_____

2 It was very difficult moving Susan by lorry and plane on her journey to Singapore.
_____

3 Congo, a male hippopotamus in Washington Zoo, was sad and lonely because Susan had left for Singapore.
_____

4 Susan was just over one year old when she left the National Zoo in Washington.
_____
etc.

Reading tests: completion

Completion items are useful in testing a student's ability to understand a reading text as well as recalling information. They can range from one-word completion answers to the completion of sentences. In many ways, items requiring the completion of sentences are very much like open-ended questions. There is little difference, for example, between the tasks involved in the two items which follow the reading extract below.

It is often very difficult indeed to build modern roads in towns and cities. Before a road in a town can be widened, a lot of buildings often have to be pulled down.

Building modern roads in many towns and cities is very hard

because _____

Why is building roads in many towns and cities very hard?

Those completion items which consist of sentences in which there are single words missing are much more objective. In other words, there is either only one correct answer for each blank or a limited number of correct answers. On the other hand, those items which require students to finish a sentence by writing several words are largely subjective and clearly more difficult to mark. For example, it will usually be necessary to take into account accuracy of written expression as well as reading comprehension. When this is the case, it is useful to allow two marks for each correct answer, one mark for a correct answer in badly written sentences, and no marks for an incorrect answer (however well the sentence has been written).

Reading texts with blanks

Note the intervals between the blanks in the following reading text. When deciding which words to omit, it is important to choose content words related to the theme or topic as well as grammar words (connectives such as *although, because,* etc. and reference words such as *he, this,* etc.) Note also in this example how the words which carry the most meaning have been omitted. The first word omitted is *bicycle* – which can only be guessed by reading on and understanding such clues as *I was riding* and *As I pedalled slowly.* Later in the text the connective *As* is omitted at the beginning of perhaps the most important sentence in the text.

I was going home on my (1) _____ at about six

o'clock on Saturday afternoon when the (2) _____

happened. I was riding on the left-hand side of the

(3) _____ near the pavement. As I pedalled slowly,

I put out my (4) _____ to turn right into Factory

Row. Then I looked behind to (5) _____ if there

---

were any cars. (6) _____ I could not see any, I began to turn right. Just as I was near the middle of the road, I (8) _____ the noise of an engine behind me. A big car was (9) _____ very fast in the middle of the road. I (10) _____ as quickly as I could, but the car also turned and (11) _____ me off my bicycle. I was thrown to one side of the road, but the (12) _____ travelled another twenty or thirty metres (13) _____ stopping. It pushed my bicycle in front of it and badly (14) _____ it.

The following example may look rather like a vocabulary test at first but further examination will show that it is a test of reading comprehension. Completing each blank is not intended to test knowledge of the meaning of the missing word. We assume, for example, that a student will know what the word *watch* means. Can the student understand the text, however, so that he or she can write the word *watch* in the blank?

LOST AND FOUND

LOST: Alpha gold (1) _____ with black strap. Has second hand. Loses 5 minutes every 24 hours. Left in Roxy Theatre, Hinkley. If found, ring 43–98621.

(1) **watch**

LOST: Penton (2) _____ with film inside. Takes excellent photographs. Reward. Ring 39972.

(2) _____

MISSING: Small black (3) _____ with white patch over ears. Barks a lot, answers to name Spot. If found, phone Lee 554778.

(3) _____

FOUND: Twelve (4) _____ for circle seats June 10 at Shenton Theatre. Tel. 755921.

(4) _____

Texts followed by summaries with blanks

The following is an example of a reading test followed by a summary of the text. Students are required to complete the summary by writing either one word or two words in each blank.

A Soviet scientist believes that a space-ship from another planet may have crashed and exploded in the Soviet Union in 1908. At the time, the explosion was so great that it was heard 1,200 kilometres away. The earth shook so violently that horses pulling a plough 400 kilometres away were thrown to the ground. Scientists say that the force of the explosion was 2,000 times greater than the first atomic bomb. Although some other scientists believe that a huge meteorite hit the earth, the Soviet scientist argues that the explosion was of nuclear origin and was probably caused by a space-ship from another world.

A scientist in the _____ now thinks that

the violent _____ in 1908 could have been

caused by a _____ . Not all scientists

_____ , however, and others think the cause

was a huge _____ . The object hit the earth

with a much more powerful force than the first

_____ .

Sometimes tables, diagrams and maps may be used in place of summaries, etc. Students have to show their understanding of a reading text by completing blanks in tables and labelling diagrams and maps.

Reading tests: cloze

Some teachers do not distinguish between blank-filling and cloze tests, using the term *cloze* for all blank-filling tests. Although cloze tests are similar in several ways to blank-filling tests, there are nevertheless basic differences between the two.

In an ordinary blank-filling test, we decide which words we will delete from a text. As we saw in the previous section, we usually choose important content words, connectives, etc. In this way, we can test a student's ability to understand specific meanings in the text.

In a cloze test, however, we never choose which words we want to omit: we delete the words systematically. First, we decide on the length of the interval between the missing words. For example, do we want to delete every fifth word or every eighth word in a text? We decide on a suitable number (usually between five and twelve) and we keep strictly to that number. If we decide to delete every seventh word, we omit every seventh word throughout the whole text – regardless of whether a particular word is unfamiliar or even whether it is someone's name. Thus there will *always* be intervals of six words between the deleted words.

For most purposes every fifth, sixth, seventh or eighth word is usually deleted from a text. If every third or fourth word is deleted, the intervals between the blanks will probably not contain enough words to enable students to understand the text. If every ninth or tenth word is deleted, students will have to read too much in order to complete only a few blanks.

A cloze test may be as long or as short as desired. In order to make a cloze test reliable, however, it is important to have a minimum number of blanks, usually forty or fifty. Thus, if we are setting an achievement or proficiency test, the reading text we choose will allow for enough blanks.

Remember that cloze tests measure students' general reading comprehension rather than their understanding of certain features in the text. Several test specialists even argue that a cloze test measures general language ability. Used for this purpose, cloze testing is very useful for assessing language proficiency in a short time and can be used for selection and proficiency purposes (but not for achievement tests). We can obtain a fairly reliable assessment in as short a time as fifteen minutes by giving a cloze test consisting of fifty blanks.

It is important to let students see the first sentence or two without any blanks. This will give them an opportunity to get used to the topic and style of the passage.

Take care not to set texts which are too difficult, especially when you are giving a progress test. Before giving a cloze test to your students, it is very important to do the test yourself (at least a day or two after you have constructed the test). You will probably be surprised how difficult it can be when you have forgotten the words which have been deleted.

When you mark the answers to a cloze test, you may count as correct either the exact word which has been deleted or any acceptable word. Research work which has been carried out on cloze testing has shown that it makes scarcely any difference whichever method is used. If the cloze test is a proficiency test or part of an examination measuring achievement, you will find it easier and quicker to count only exact words as correct – especially if a large number of students have taken the test. However, if the cloze test is part of a progress test, you may wish to mark any acceptable answer (i.e. synonyms) as correct – unless you specially want students to use certain words which they have learnt in your previous lessons. On the whole, it is more encouraging for students to know that their answers are regarded as correct if they have used appropriate synonyms. This is an important point to bear in mind when you go through your students' answers in class.

Cloze testing is most useful when used for its original purpose: to measure the reading difficulty level of a text. For example, if you wish to find out whether a reading book is at a suitable level for your students, take an extract (about 400 or 500 words) from it and use it as a cloze test by deleting every seventh word. After giving the test to the class, find out the average percentage mark scored by the class. (Add up all the scores of the class and divide by the number of students in the class. Then express this score as a percentage.)

If the average mark of the class is above 53 per cent, the reading book can be used by students working on their own: the score is called the *independent level*. If the average mark is between 44 and 53 per cent, the book is suitable for use with a class and the teacher: this range of marks is called the *instructional level*. If the average mark is below 44 per cent, the book is far too difficult to use even with the teacher; this score is thus referred to as the *frustrational level*.

Testing reading with other skills

Reading is often tested together with other skills in performance-referenced tests. The skill with which reading is most closely related in many tests is writing. Frequently, reading is used to provide a stimulus for writing: for example, students may be instructed to write a reply to a certain letter. Clearly, they must be able to read and understand the letter before they can reply to it. In addition to providing a basis for writing, reading frequently plays an integral part of the writing task itself. If students are required to complete an application form as part of a writing test, it will be necessary for them to understand the information and instructions contained in the form.

At a more advanced level, students may be required to read a text in order to take notes. However, it is project work which usually makes most use of multi-mode reading tests. In a project which requires students to make decisions with regard to alternative forms of energy, for example, discussions and report writing will be based on a considerable amount of initial reading. Such a variety of tasks will enable you to assess your students' performances not only in reading but also in speaking and writing (and also possibly in listening). Although not given as formal tests, such activities in a project will usually enable accurate and reliable assessments to be made.

Always attempt to give realistic tasks for students to perform in such tests. Avoid traditional kinds of tests in which students are instructed simply to read a text and talk about it. Instead, give a task which students might actually perform in real life, asking them to read some instructions, for example, and explain them to a younger brother or sister.

Activities

1

Complete the following test item by writing three options for each of the ten multiple-choice items shown. As the correct option has been given in every case, you should write only two distractors and vary the position of the correct option. Note that the first two items have been done to help you to start.

A: What's the (1) _____ going to be like tomorrow?

B: The (2) _____ for tomorrow isn't too good.

A: It's going to be quite cool with (3) _____ as low as 18°C.

B: But are we going to have any rain?

A: Not a lot. It'll be (4) _____ over most of the country but there may be a few (5) _____ in the morning. In the north, it's going to be (6) _____ all day with only one or two sunny (7) _____. It's also going to rain (8) _____ there in the evening. In fact, the rain's going to (9) _____ across the country overnight.

B: Well, I suppose it could be worse.

A: I don't know. It's going to be very (10) _____, too.

1 A weather   B climate   C condition
2 A news   B prophesy C forecast
3 temperatures
4 fine
5 showers
6 cloudy
7 periods
8 heavily
9 spread
10 windy

2

Each of the following multiple-choice items is based on the accompanying reading passage and consists of three options. However, each item provides an example of a fault described in this section. Say what the fault is and then re-write the item, correcting the fault.

After you have done this, discuss your items with a colleague. Then say which of the multiple-choice items might be better as open-ended questions.

Many people are afraid of snakes and try their best to kill them whenever they can. However, snakes attack human beings only when they are disturbed. Unfortunately, few people know that a snake's tongue is not dangerous. It is simply for touching things and for smelling substances. A snake's poison flows through its fangs which are really hollow teeth. If you are bitten by a snake, you should keep calm, remember the snake's colour and see a doctor at once.

1 A lot of people kill snakes because
    A snakes are very dangerous creatures.
    B they are frightened of them.
    C they think snakes will harm them.

2 Snakes attack human beings
    A only when someone startles them.
    B whenever they feel very hungry.
    C never.

3 A snake uses its forked tongue
    A to taste food.
    B to smell things.
    C to touch things.

4 When a snake bites a person or an animal, the poison flows through
    A its tongue.
    B the hollow teeth in its upper jaw.
    C its body.

5 When a snake bites you, you should try to
    A catch it and take it with you to the nearest doctor.
    B remember its colour and quickly see a doctor.
    C kill the snake as quickly as you can.

3

Write a true/false reading test based on any book which students are reading. Write twelve true/false items and then add three items under the class *not stated*. Finally, write suitable instructions for this test.

4

Read the following newspaper report and then do these tasks:

  i) Delete ten words in the text and replace them with blanks. (Re-write part of the report if you think it is necessary.)

ii) Write a summary or short paraphrase of the report, omitting *either* single words *or* phrases and clauses.

Sixteen Die in Flash Flood

Latest reports from the north-east provinces state that at least sixteen people lost their lives in Saturday's floods. A further nine people, mostly children, are reported missing, believed dead.

The floods occurred a few hours after heavy rain in the north. Water poured down the steep mountain sides, causing a series of landslides. Streams and rivers overflowed their banks in several places. Three villages were totally destroyed and another was badly damaged. More than 2,000 people are now homeless as a result.

Rescue teams using helicopters and boats have been working non-stop for the past twenty-four hours. Most of the homeless villagers were taken by ambulance to nearby towns. However, a few have refused to leave their homes and are sitting on rooftops waiting for the water to go down.

More heavy rain is forecast for tomorrow. The government is arranging to evacuate other villages in the area in case of further flooding.

5

Try to obtain any newspaper (or book) written in English. Choose a short extract from it and write a cloze test, omitting every seventh word. Put the cloze test on one side and try to do it a week later.

Discussion

1 Draw up a list of suitable vocabulary items to include in a progress test for your class. Discuss your reasons for selecting the items for inclusion.

2 Discuss the merits and drawbacks of writing multiple-choice tests of reading.

3 What are some of the difficulties of marking reading tests in which students are required to write out their answers to questions?

4 Are there any levels at which cloze tests are unsuitable? Discuss with a colleague.

Testing writing skills

Grammar and Structure

Multiple-choice items

Remember that multiple-choice items test an ability to *recognise* sentences which are grammatically correct. This ability is not the same as the ability to *produce* correct sentences. If you remember this limitation, you can still find multiple-choice items useful for certain purposes, especially in progress tests. They are especially useful for finding out more about the difficulties which students have with certain areas of grammar.

A multiple-choice item must have only one correct answer. This seems to be common sense, but it is very easy to write an item with two correct answers without realising it. The following item, for example, has two correct answers: *A* as well as the expected answer *C*.

How _____ sugar do you take in your coffee?
  A little B few C much D many

All the options in a multiple-choice item should be at the same level of difficulty:

The car was full of _____ .
  A petrol B a petrol C the petrol D some petrol

Wherever possible, set the items in context. The disadvantage of using a passage for a progress or an achievement test is simply that you may be prevented from choosing certain particular areas of grammar on which to concentrate, especially if the passage is fairly short. For example, it will be very difficult to find one or two short paragraphs which will enable you to have ten items testing the use of the present perfect tense, six items testing the use of articles before uncountable nouns, etc. When you choose a paragraph, you can test only the grammatical points which occur in that paragraph.

If you want to concentrate on a certain area of grammar, put the item into a short two-line dialogue. This is better than providing no context at all. Thus, the item

_____ a pen and a piece of paper.
  A I like   B I'll like   C I'd like   D I'm liking

becomes more meaningful when expressed as a reply to a request:

'Can I get you anything?'
'_____ a pen and a piece of paper, please.'
  A I like   B I'll like   C I'd like   D I'm liking

As in multiple-choice testing of vocabulary and reading, it is often unnecessary to write four options for your items: three options are enough in most classroom tests.

Finally, remember that certain areas of grammar do not lend themselves to the multiple-choice format. Thus, an ability to use articles (*a, an, the*) and concord (the agreement between subject and verb, etc.) is much better tested in other ways.

Error-recognition items

Use the errors your students make in their compositions to write these types of items. The first example below is really a multiple-choice item. In the item, four words or phrases are underlined and marked A, B, C and D. Students must choose the underlined word or phrase which is incorrect.

---

1 It was a terrible accident at an air-show held in
  A   B   C   D
West Germany yesterday.

2 One of the aircraft was crashed into two other aircraft
          A   B   C
during the display.
  D

3 There was wreckage everywhere and hundred of people
        A   B   C
were killed or badly injured.
                    D

etc.

The following example illustrates another way of writing this type of item. Students are told there is a mistake in grammar in each sentence and instructed to write the letter of that part of the sentence in which it occurs.

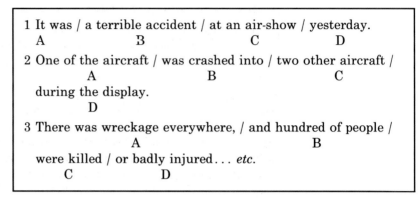

1 It was / a terrible accident / at an air-show / yesterday.
  A   B   C   D

2 One of the aircraft / was crashed into / two other aircraft /
        A   B   C
  during the display.
        D

3 There was wreckage everywhere, / and hundred of people /
             A   B
  were killed / or badly injured... *etc.*
    C   D

This latter type of item is more useful for testing errors caused by omission, especially those caused by the omission of the article.

Another way of presenting this type of item is simply to give students incorrect sentences and ask them to write out the correct version. It is helpful if you inform them that there is only one mistake in each sentence – otherwise many students will try to change every part of the sentence even though there may be no mistakes at all. Unfortunately, even if students correct a mistake, they may make errors in copying out the sentence. We are then faced with problems of marking.

Re-arrangement

In the following example students are required to unscramble sentences. They must write out each sentence, putting the words and phrases in their correct order. As you will see, this type of item is useful for testing an awareness of the order of adjectives, the position of adverbs, inversion and several other areas of grammar.

1 She was wearing a ....
  new / jacket / leather / red / lovely

2 Susan ....
  the phone / when / already / rang / suddenly / finished / had

3 I asked her if ....
   anyone / she / to help / find / us / could /

4 I made Alan ....
   his parents / to / the broken bicycle / show

5 Not only ....
   also / Dave / forgot / his homework / come / to bring /
   late / but / did / he

By requiring students to re-arrange sentences, you encourage them to pay careful attention to such grammatical markers as connectives (*since, but, although, however, consequently*, etc.) and pronouns. These usually provide important clues to the correct order of the sentences. In the following example, students can be instructed to re-write the four sentences in the correct order or simply to put the letters of each sentence (A, B, C, D) in the correct order.

A However, we decided to set out and try to climb the mountain.
B This time we had better climbing equipment and were determined to succeed.
C Several people in the group had tried this before but no one had managed to get to the top.
D There was a strong wind and it was raining very heavily.

Changing words

A completely different type of question requires students to put verbs into their correct tense or voice. This question is quite easy and straightforward to construct. However, it is important to provide an interesting context.

I said that if I (1) to discover the fire	(1) _____
earlier, I (2) to succeed in	(2) _____
(3) to extinguish it before it	(3) _____
(4) to catch hold	(4) _____
etc.	

Blank-filling

The same principles apply to the use of blanks for testing grammar as for vocabulary. In a test of grammar, however, it is important to choose the words to omit very carefully so that they are all grammatical words (e.g. *to, in, is, the*). Once again, avoid writing separate sentences; blank-filling items should consist of paragraphs providing an interesting and relevant context. Notice the lay-out of the following test item; it makes it easy for students to do and easy for you to mark.

It is interesting (1) _____ note that	(1) _____
(2) _____ was an extremely close connection	(2) _____
(3) _____ playing cards, paper money and	(3) _____
gambling. Early Chinese cards, (4) _____	(4) _____
instance, bear (5) _____ close resemblance	(5) _____
(6) _____ early Chinese paper money.	(6) _____
etc.	

A slightly different form of blank-filling item requires students to insert only grammatical or functional words. This time, however, no blank spaces are inserted in the text. The aim is to give students the task of finding out not only which words have been omitted but where they have been omitted. As you will know from your experience of correcting students' written work, many errors are caused by the omission of auxiliary verbs, the introductory pronouns *there* and *it*, articles and prepositions. In the item, students are told that one word has been omitted on each line. They are instructed to put a stroke (/) where the word has been omitted and to write the missing word in the appropriate blank.

1 _____	The heaviest man in world was
2 _____	Jon Brower Minnoch. He born in 1941
3 _____	and weighed more 635 kilograms
4 _____	when he was young man.
etc.	

Controlled writing

Control over what students write in an exam may range from very strict control over the grammar and forms of language used to less strict control over the functions and subject-matter. The following types of questions show the range of control and some of the forms it can take.

Transformation

Items which involve re-writing sentences according to certain patterns are more suitable for use in intermediate and advanced tests than in tests at an elementary level.

---

1 No other living plant grows so tall and so fast as bamboo.

Bamboo _____

2 A stalk of Japan's commonest bamboo has grown over a metre in only twenty-four hours.
It has taken _____

3 Bamboo is peculiar in several respects.

Bamboo has _____
etc.

It is also possible to get students to do a similar task by giving them a word in brackets instead of the beginning of the new sentence. The use of the word given will automatically involve re-writing the sentence. The chief weakness with this type of item is the lack of context. It is practically impossible to provide a context for items involving the re-writing of sentences.

---

1   It is not necessary to answer all the questions. (*need*)

_____

2   His angry outburst was completely unexpected. (*took*)

_____
etc.

Broken sentences

You can test a student's ability to write sentences from a series of words and phrases. Used in this way, the following type of question can be very useful for testing controlled writing skills. Students are required to make whatever changes are necessary to form good sentences, adding articles, prepositions, etc. and putting verbs in their correct tense. When you write this type of question, try to put the 'broken sentences' in the form of a paragraph, a dialogue or a letter. The question will then appear more relevant and meaningful to the student.

Dear Cindy,
Thanks / lot / your letter / which / arrive / yesterday.

1 _____

Congratulations / pass / your entrance exams.

2 _____

You / work / very hard / past year / but now / it / all / be / worthwhile.

3 _____

I wonder / if / you / like / stay / me / few days.

4 _____

It / be / good / see / you / and hear / all / news.

5 _____

I look forward / hear / you / very soon.

6 _____
Best wishes,
    Cathy

Sentence and paragraph completion

Some items require students to complete sentences or paragraphs. In this way, writing is integrated with reading comprehension and becomes a more realistic task.

> Most of the students in my class were rather lazy and did not enjoy the course. Some even stayed away from school quite often . Pauline, however, _____
>
> _____
>
> *etc.*

Other blank-filling items take the form of incomplete dialogues.

> A: _____
>
> B: So do I. I generally watch for an hour or two every evening.
>
> A: _____
>
> B: Immediately after I've finished my homework at about eight.
>
> A: _____
>
> B: So are mine. The funnier, the better.
> *etc.*

Form-filling

This is a very relevant task for students: in modern life it is often necessary for students to fill in forms. For example, students may be given an application form for a summer school in Britain. They are asked to give details about themselves.

Notes and diaries

One advantage of using notes as a basis for free writing lies in the control provided. By controlling what students write to some degree, you can ensure that certain grammatical patterns and language functions are tested. Another advantage of using notes lies in the fact that they ensure all students perform a similar writing task. When students are given the same task, their attempts can be compared fairly with one another.

The following is an example of the use of notes as a stimulus for writing.

You have just attended a short talk on choosing places to go for a holiday. Below are the notes which you have taken. Using the information in the notes, complete the four sentences, giving your reasons.

SWITZERLAND

by coach to Interlaken
can climb mountains
relaxing
beautiful scenery
interesting tours
excellent hotel with
   swimming pool
good food
some good shops

SPAIN

excellent beaches
plenty of sun
   (but very hot)
swimming, fishing, golf
discos at night
frequent direct flights
quite cheap
see a bull-fight
friends going

I would prefer to go for a holiday to _____
because _____
When I arrived there, I would be able to _____
_____
However, if I didn't go there, I would go to _____
because _____
I think I would enjoy _____
_____

Diary entries are also useful for providing a stimulus for free writing. Students use the information in the diary to write a letter to a friend. They can be asked to fill in any days which have been left blank in the diary. In this way, students can have a chance to show any creative writing ability which they may have.

1	MONDAY	Holiday! Go swimming
2	TUESDAY	Holiday! Study!
3	WEDNESDAY	Exams start.

4	THURSDAY	
5	FRIDAY	Exams finish. Go to cinema.
6	SATURDAY	
7	SUNDAY	Visit Uncle Ken

Free writing

The only really satisfactory way to assess a student's ability to write is by means of a composition test. Setting composition exams is reasonably straightforward provided that you remember a few basic principles.

Choosing subjects

Firstly, choose subjects which are within the experience of your students. Avoid very general, abstract topics such as 'The Countryside At Night', 'The Importance Of Time', 'Great Advances Our Country Has Made', etc. Clear and precise titles help students to focus their thoughts and direct their ideas. It is useful to give brief descriptions of everyday situations which are meaningful for students.

> A cousin of yours from another part of your country is coming to stay with you for a week. Your cousin is very interested in cycling and swimming. Tell him or her what you plan to do and where you plan to go. Arrange to meet your cousin at the local bus or train station. Unfortunately, you and your cousin last saw each other ten years ago, when you where both much younger. Describe what you look like and how you can be recognised. Whereabouts at the station will you meet?

Realistic writing tasks

Think about the likely contexts in which your students will write. Most people write letters in their daily lives; few write compositions! Therefore, test your students' ability to write letters (similar to that in the previous example). Other common writing tasks include messages (especially phone messages) and notes. At the intermediate and advanced levels, students will often find themselves in situations in which they are required to write reports: for example, a report of a school visit, a report on a person, a laboratory report, etc. If English is used as a medium of instruction in schools in your country, relate the writing contexts to the other subjects in the school (e.g. descriptions of experiments, accounts of battles, etc.). Even if English is not used as the means of instruction, try to get students to do such writing tasks in English – and include such tasks in the test from time to time. In this way, students will experience writing English for a relevant purpose.

Writing for a purpose

Always try to give your students a purpose for writing, even in a classroom test. This is important for motivating students and encouraging them to produce good written work. Few people ever write in real life without a definite purpose.

Writing for an audience

It is helpful if students know for whom they are writing. Knowing who our readers are influences the way in which we write. Scientists, for example, will write a report for other scientists in a different way from the way they will write for non-specialists. In writing instructions for a composition or a letter, therefore, try to be as specific as you can and give details about the person or people to whom the student is writing.

Specific instructions

The following is an example of an instruction which is very specific and contains enough detail about the people and the situation to be used as a basis for the writing task.

A schoolfriend of yours is staying with his or her parents in their small holiday house 100 kilometres away on the coast. Your friend has just written to invite you to join him or her for a week and has asked what you would like to do on your short holiday. Write a reply, accepting his or her invitation and saying what you would like to do. You like cycling and swimming but your friend is keen on walking and climbing.

Your friend likes to get up early to do things each day. On the other hand, you like to relax on holiday and get up late. You like to sit on a beach and read a good book. You are also keen on photography.

Such an instruction emphasises the communicative nature of language learning far more than a short, general instruction like the following:

Write a letter to a schoolfriend of yours, accepting an invitation to spend a week's holiday with him or her on the coast. Say what you would like to do on your holiday.

Using pictures for writing

In everyday life your students may sometimes be required to describe people, objects, places, and even processes. There will also be times when they will have to write about sequences of events, incidents, etc. and give directions. Pictures provide students with ideas for such tasks, enabling them to give their full attention to using the written language.

The control which pictures exert over the content of the written work is also useful in another way. We can easily tell what students want to write and we can thus measure their success in achieving this goal. If students fail to write about the contents of a picture, we have good reason for suspecting that it is because they feel unable to use the language necessary for this purpose.

Pictures are now being used increasingly in many public exams. You may want to use pictures to do any of the following tasks in your test:

1 to describe a scene, object or person
2 to compare two scenes, etc.
3 to tell a story
4 to give instructions or directions
5 to describe a process.

You can easily use suitable pictures from picture composition books and from magazines, newspapers and comics. When you use pictures from any source at all (especially from books published in another country), however, make sure that your students can understand the pictures without any difficulty. There are often cultural difficulties which may be overlooked. When using pictures for teaching, you can anticipate such difficulties and prepare for them. When testing, however, you cannot do this for obvious reasons and you must choose the pictures for the test much more carefully.

Moreover, students below a certain age may sometimes have difficulty in understanding such parts of a picture as aerial views, perspective, cause-and-effect relationships, etc. Seeing and understanding what is in a picture can be just as difficult as reading what is in a text.

Marking compositions

When you mark a student's composition, you should take care to mark only what the student has written. Although this advice seems to be common sense, it is often all too easy to be influenced by other factors in addition to the quality of the written work. To start with, try not to look at the student's name on the test paper. A lot of teachers award marks according to their knowledge of the student rather than what the student has written. It is also easy to be influenced by handwriting. Although good handwriting is undoubtedly important, you should not allow your assessment of the general quality of the student's written work to be influenced unduly by handwriting.

There are three chief methods of marking compositions:
1 the error-count method,
2 the analytic method, and
3 the impression (or multiple-marking) method.

The error-count method
The error-count method involves counting up the number of errors which a student has made and deducting this number from a possible maximum total. However, this method usually fails to take into account that some errors are more serious than others, especially at certain stages of learning English.

Most important of all, however, this method completely ignores content. Indeed, by concentrating entirely on the more negative aspects of using language, it ignores the real purpose of writing: communication. Just imagine writing a letter to one of your friends. How much would you write if you knew that your friend was going to mark every mistake you made? How often would you *want* to write to your friend?

As a result, the error-count method is not recommended even if an additional mark is given for the content of the piece of writing.

The analytic method

A much better method of marking is the analytic method. This method is particularly useful for class progress tests when you want to inform your students about their performances. First identify the features which you want to mark. For example, you may be interested in the following areas: fluency, grammar, vocabulary, content, spelling. Give each of these areas an appropriate mark out of a total of 5 or 6.

Then draw up a grid or table and put a cross in each appropriate square when you mark a composition (as shown in the example). Note that the maximum total number of marks for fluency is 5 and the minimum is 1. The maximum total number of marks for all 5 sections is 25 (i.e. 5 × 5) and the minimum is 5 (i.e. 5 × 1).

	5	4	3	2	1
Fluency			X		
Grammar		X			
Vocabulary				X	
Content	X				
Spelling			X		

Finally, total the marks which you have given in the table:
e.g. 3 (fluency) + 4 (grammar) + 2 (vocabulary) + 5 (content) +
3 (spelling) = 17/25.

If you want to emphasise a certain feature in the table, you can
double that particular mark. For example, you may want to
emphasise to your class the importance of correct use of
language, especially if you find many students write interesting
and relevant compositions which are marred by careless errors. In
this case, simply double the score (4) for grammar. Your marks
will thus read: 3 (fluency) + 8 (grammar) + 2 (vocabulary) +
5 (content) + 3 (spelling) = 21/30.

If you want to reduce the weighting of any section, simply draw
lines through the relevant part in the table. For example, if you
want to give less importance to spelling in your marking, you
might want to mark this section out of 2. The table would then
appear as follows:

	5	4	3	2	1
Fluency			X		
Grammar		X			
Vocabulary				X	
Content	X				
Spelling	/////	/////	/////		X

The total marks would now be: 3+4+2+5+1 = 15/22

It is sometimes helpful to write brief notes for the different levels
of each category (probably at the beginning of the school term or
year).

(Note that in the following example the section on Content has
been omitted on account of space.)

Fluency	5	Flowing style – very easy to understand – both complex and simple sentences – very effective
	4	Quite flowing style – mostly easy to understand – a few complex sentences – effective
	3	Style reasonably smooth – not too hard to understand – mostly (but not all) simple sentences – fairly effective
	2	Jerky style – an effort needed to understand and enjoy – complex sentences confusing – mostly simple sentences or compound sentences
	1	Very jerky – hard to understand – cannot enjoy reading – almost all simple sentences – complex sentences confusing – excessive use of 'and'
Grammar	5	Mastery of grammar taught on course – only 1 or 2 minor mistakes
	4	A few minor mistakes only (prepositions, articles, etc.)
	3	Only 1 or 2 major mistakes but a few minor ones
	2	Major mistakes which lead to difficulty in understanding – lack of mastery of sentence construction
	1	Numerous serious mistakes – no mastery of sentence construction – almost unintelligible
Vocabulary	5	Use of wide range of vocabulary taught previously
	4	Good use of new words acquired – use of appropriate synonyms, circumlocution, etc.
	3	Attempts to use words acquired – fairly appropriate vocabulary on the whole but sometimes restricted – has to resort to use of synonyms, circumlocution, etc. on a few occasions
	2	Restricted vocabulary – use of synonyms (but not always appropriate) – imprecise and vague – affects meaning
	1	Very restricted vocabulary – inappropriate use of synonyms – seriously hinders communication
Spelling	5	No errors
	4	1 or 2 minor errors only (e.g. ie or ei)
	3	Several errors – do not interfere significantly with communication – not too hard to understand
	2	Several errors – some interfere with communication – some words very hard to recognise
	1	Numerous errors – hard to recognise several words – communication made very difficult

The impression method

Impression marking, sometimes called multiple-marking, is a useful method of marking a large number of compositions, especially in public tests and end-of-year school tests. As the name suggests, the score is based on the marker's total impression of the composition as a whole. When you use this method, you *glance* at each composition. Don't read it. In fact, once you find yourself *reading* a composition, it is a sign that you are growing tired and you should stop marking at this point.

Using this method of marking, you can usually mark up to twenty scripts an hour – possibly more if they are fairly short. Thus, marking is very quick and reliable provided that three markers glance through each composition. For school tests, however, two markers are often enough.

It is important for the two or three markers to mark a sample number of scripts first (probably ten or twenty) and compare their marks. Eventually everyone should agree on appropriate scores to award. In the few cases where markers disagree later in their marking, the appropriate compositions are put on one side and *read* by all three markers. Brief discussions then take place and final scores are agreed by the markers.

Note that, for multiple-marking purposes, compositions are often marked on a scale of 5 or 6.

The following table shows the scores which three markers have given for four compositions.

	Comp 1	Comp 2	Comp 3	Comp 4
Marker A	2	1	4	2
Marker B	3	2	5	4
Marker C	3	1	3	1
Total	8	4	12	7

The three markers clearly disagree about Composition 4. Marker B is looking for something quite different from Marker C. Perhaps Marker B is influenced by handwriting and neatness. Perhaps Markers A and C are marking for successful communication while Marker B may be marking for grammatical accuracy. The total score of 7 seems to be fair in reflecting the differences. If this composition is read and discussed, however, the score will probably be even more reliable and fair.

Remember that impression marking is useful for tests in which a lot of students have taken part. It is not satisfactory for class progress tests since it will not enable you to tell students why they have obtained a certain score and what their areas of weakness are.

Testing writing with other skills

As we saw in the previous chapter, the reading and writing skills are often tested in combination with each other, especially in performance-referenced tests. When devising such multi-mode tests, however, care should be taken to avoid giving tasks in which students simply copy out large parts of a reading text in their written work. If you think that students will be able to perform part of the writing task simply by reproducing the reading text, then another kind of task should be given or else the writing task should be given separately on its own.

When you set multi-mode tests of writing, think of the various tasks students may be required to perform in real life. Instead of instructing students to listen to a conversation and write a summary of what has been said, try to identify a possible situation in which students may find it necessary to write out something which they have heard: e.g. listening to (and seeing) a demonstration of how to do something and then writing out the various steps, etc.

Activities

1
Look carefully at the letter in the box on page 114. Then choose any five errors as a basis for writing the following kinds of test items:

1 5 multiple-choice grammar items
2 5 error-recognition items
3 5 blank-filling items (with blank spaces)

4 5 blank-filling items (with oblique strokes and with one word omitted on each line)

Dear Sharon,

We are having the good holiday at Southend. It is a pretty town and we are liking it very much. Today it is very hot and sunny here but when we arrived to Brinley on Saturday it was a very bad storm. The weather changed now and the forecast for the rest of week is very good.

Yesterday morning I have gone swimming. As you know, I used to diving a lot but last year I hit the head on a small rock. Now my father will not let me to dive even if water is very deep. Still, I enjoy to swim and play about in the water.

By the way, I just have started to play the tennis. It's a very good game. The hotel where we are staying there has two tennis courts. It is also a small golf course near to the hotel and my father says he will teach me how to play. It is several years ago since he plays, and so I don't think he would be very good! I hope I would beat him!

The next time we come here you must to come with us. I am looking forward to see you again soon.

                  With best wishes,

                      Dan

2

Design a form for students to complete in a test. Imagine that they are required to complete an application for a library ticket. You will want to know the following details:

their name, address, age, etc.

the name (and position) of someone who will promise to

replace any books they may lose

their school and class/place of work and position

their interests or favourite subject

details about their education

reasons for joining and any suggestions they may have

3

Read the following general instructions for writing a letter and two compositions. Then re-write the instructions to provide more communicative writing tasks.

---

1 Write a letter to try to persuade your cousin to come to your party and stay overnight at your house.

2 Describe your best friend.

3 Write about something unusual which has happened to you.

4

Look at six compositions which have been written recently by your own students. Work in groups of three or four if possible. First use the impression method to mark all six compositions. Then use the analytic method to mark them, drawing up your own table. Do the two different scores for each of the six compositions agree with each other?

Discussion

1 Study any test of grammar which you have used. What kind of items were used? Could the test be improved by using different item types?

2 What types of simple everyday writing tasks may your students be required to perform in English or in their mother tongue? Discuss ways in which these could be incorporated in a test of writing.

3 Choose any picture and discuss its usefulness as a basis for a test of writing.

4 Describe in detail your own method of marking free written work. What are the advantages and disadvantages of this method?

Continuous assessment

General

Continuous assessment is a procedure which enables you to assess over a period of weeks or months those aspects of a student's performance which cannot normally be assessed as satisfactorily by means of tests. For example, you can use continuous assessment to measure students' work in groups and their overall progress as shown in class. Continuous assessment includes marks or grades for homework as well as scores on classroom tests.

Most students like continuous assessment, but it may still be stressful if you do not handle it carefully. There will usually be less stress, for example, if you tell students that their worst three assignments will not be taken into account in awarding a final score or grade.

Continuous assessment enables us to take into account certain qualities which cannot be assessed in any other way: namely, effort, persistence and attitude. You can draw up short tables to enable you to grade very broadly what you wish to measure (provided that you are aware of the limitations of measuring such qualities).

The following table provides an example of a teacher's attempts to grade students according to their persistence and determination in learning English.

| 5 | Most persistent and thorough in all class and homework assignments. Interested in learning and keen to do well. |
| 4 | Persistent and thorough on the whole. Usually works well in class and mostly does homework conscientiously. Fairly keen. |

3	Not too persistent but mostly tries. Average work in class and does homework (but never more than necessary). Interested on the whole but not too keen.
2	Soon loses interest. Sometimes tries but finds it hard to concentrate for long in class. Sometimes forgets to do homework or does only part of homework.
1	Lacks interest. Dislikes learning English. Cannot concentrate for long and often fails to do homework.

When you start to write your own table, try to imagine the student who always tries the hardest and let him or her be the model for your description of the top grade. Then imagine the laziest and least motivated student (if you have such a student!) and write an appropriate description of the bottom grade. Then imagine the average student, and so on.

Remember that a positive attitude to learning is very important indeed and should constantly be encouraged – either through some kind of formal grading or, preferably, by means of indirect and informal encouragement.

Oral activities: projects and role play

In addition to the qualities referred to in the previous section of this chapter, there are certain language skills which cannot be suitably assessed by formal methods of testing. Continuous assessment enables us to see how students can perform in situations and assignments which are closer to real life than formal examinations. Since language (particularly oral language) is essentially a communicative activity, it follows that the oral skills can best be measured by observing how students use language amongst themselves to achieve certain goals.

Spontaneous conversation – genuine communication – is extremely difficult to examine. In many oral tests examiners ask students questions to which they already know the answer. Often an examiner will still be in a position of asking questions simply for the sake of asking questions. In short, the whole situation is artificial; there is too much control and there is nothing spontaneous.

Since it is always essential to give students a reason for speaking, we should devise suitable activities with this in mind. For example, if we want students to exchange information in as natural a way as possible, we can give each student (or each group of students) only part of the information they need. Immediately they will be in the position of asking questions to which they do not know the answer. They themselves will then be asked in turn about the information which they have and the others lack. Such situations are not too difficult to devise. Simply divide students into pairs or let them work in small groups of three or four and give each student an incomplete text or diagram. The students then exchange information orally, listening carefully in order to complete the text or diagram and telling the other students about the contents of their own text or diagram.

Simple role playing is also an activity useful for continuous assessment purposes. Students can act various parts and are given details about a certain situation. For example, a student may be told to buy certain things in a shop but he or she may not be given enough money to get all the things. Another student will be told to act the part of the shopkeeper. While the shopkeeper is serving the customer, another person comes in the shop. The other person is in a great hurry and only wants something small.

This is just one example of a possible situation which students can act out. It is important at the outset to give students in a role play a clear idea of who they are, what they are like and what they should do. Avoid letting them spend a long time preparing for the role play. Students should have the opportunity to speak spontaneously and to react to something unexpected.

While this oral activity is taking place, walk round the class from group to group. Jot down one or two notes discreetly about certain students. Use a card or small note pad. Never make it obvious that you are assessing the students in any way. And don't try to observe every student. Restrict your observations to a handful of students in each lesson – say, six or seven.

When supervising and assessing such activities, it is not necessary for you to remain aloof and provide no help at all. Your active involvement in an activity from time to time can be very useful provided that you take care not to dominate the entire activity.

Whatever the kind of activity, you should try to be systematic in keeping records of your students' progress. Small cards are always very useful as they enable you to walk around the class from group to group, jotting down brief comments and, where appropriate, indications of grades. Remember, however, that short notes are usually far more informative for your purposes than grades or scores. In formal tests we are concerned frequently (but not always) with quantitative assessments (e.g. 24 out of 30, 63 per cent, B−, etc). In continuous assessment, however, we should be far more concerned with qualitative judgements. One or two sentences − or short notes − will usually tell us far more about a student than a numerical score.

Writing: editing and group activities

In ordinary writing tests we rarely allow for students' editing skills − the skills of correcting what they have written, re-organising it, omitting certain parts, adding other parts and generally expressing themselves more effectively. When we administer tests of writing, we usually expect students to be able to write a perfect piece of prose at their very first attempt. Such a task is one which few professional writers ever achieve or even attempt to achieve.

This situation is usually a result of the fact that the assessment of the editing skills is not particularly suited to normal testing situations. These skills are far better measured in class by careful observation whenever students are engaged in a writing task; hence the importance of continuous assessment in this field.

Unfortunately, most tests also require students to write a composition, letter, report, etc. within strict time limits. Once again, such tests do not reflect the situations so often encountered in real life, when we have considerable time to write and re-write. Consequently, in many cases you will find that continuous assessment is a much better tool for the measurement of writing than either a formal or an informal test.

Group writing activities also especially lend themselves to continuous assessment. In a group task, each individual student writes a paragraph or part of a composition. Then, working together as a group, the students organise the different paragraphs into a complete composition. As they do this, they check each part for errors. Finally, after discussion and re-writing at this stage, all the students in the group write out the complete composition – an activity which can be judged satisfactorily only by means of continuous assessment.

Using questions for continuous assessment

Questions have several purposes in teaching and testing. We are chiefly concerned here with 1) finding out students' strengths and weaknesses, 2) evaluating students' preparation, and 3) checking comprehension.

When you use questions as an aid to assessment, don't jot down marks and comments in front of the class. Before you ask questions, choose only three or four students for observation. After your questions (or preferably at the end of the lesson), quickly write down one or two notes about the students concerned. Students should never be aware that you are asking questions to assess them in any way. Questioning should be a pleasant experience with as great an emphasis on helping students to learn as on assessing their progress and diagnosing their weaknesses.

Consequently, always ask questions in a friendly and sympathetic manner. Moreover, vary the difficulty level of your questions to suit both more able and less able students.

Many of the questions you ask in teaching English may be divided into the following types:

1 recognition questions
   Did the girl in the story you've just read go on a picnic or stay at home?

2 recall questions
   What did the girl do in the story you've just read?

3 comprehension questions
   Can you tell me what the author's reasons for his view were?

4 evaluation questions
What's your opinion about the way Tina acted when she heard the news?

5 application questions
The word 'edible' refers to any kind of food which isn't poisonous. What would you do if you found some berries which you knew were inedible?

It isn't necessary to vary your questions systematically according to the types exemplified here. It is enough to be aware of the different kinds of questions and to try to vary them from time to time. Concentrate on forming a reliable impression of a student and on noting down general information about the student's performance.

Combining methods

Remember that the most reliable form of continuous assessment combines grades and comments from course work, projects and group work, homework assignments, oral questioning, and progress tests.

Moreover, in many schools and colleges the information obtained from continuous assessment is further combined with terminal assessment i.e. marks in an end-of-term or end-of-year exam. Once you feel confident about the reliability of the grades you award in your continuous assessment of students, you may wish to dispense with terminal assessment or at least reduce the number of formal exams.

Continuous assessment should be regarded as an integral part of your teaching and your students' learning. Above all, it should be designed and administered so that it forms a pleasant component of your teaching programme. Often students will be quite unaware of any kind of assessment taking place since the whole situation will be informal and relaxed. If continuous assessment is treated as a formal means of student measurement in any way at all, its value will be largely lost.

If carried out sensibly, continuous assessment will be as natural a process as learning itself and indistinguishable from it. One of its main purposes will, in fact, be to improve your teaching by providing opportunities for recall and revision. Another equally important purpose will be to provide you with a means of diagnosing not only your students' weaknesses but any weaknesses in your teaching, in your particular programme of work, in the books you use and in the syllabus you are following. In short, it will tell you more about your own teaching.

Above all, however, continuous assessment should encourage learning and motivate students. This, after all, should be the reason for everything we do when we teach and test in the classroom.

Student self-evaluation

An important means of continuous assessment takes the form of student self-evaluation. Students are asked to assess themselves each week according to the most appropriate grades listed on a simple form. The students then show you their forms at the end of the week and briefly discuss their results individually with you. Whenever possible, you can compare your own grades with the grades which students have awarded themselves. Each individual interview will usually take no more than one or two minutes except in rare cases where there is a great discrepancy between a student's self-appraisal and your own view.

Sometimes part of the first lesson the following week can be spent on discussions of the completed forms. Other students' views are now elicited on certain individual performances, as appropriate.

Note that the weekly self-evaluation may include all the skills (reflecting all the learning that has taken place) or may concentrate on only one skill or area of language, depending on the type of course given. If it concentrates on only one skill, however, make sure that progress in a different skill is evaluated by students each week e.g. Week 1 listening; Week 2 writing; Week 3 speaking; and Week 4 reading.

The following are two examples of forms which can be used for student self-evaluation of listening and writing skills. Note that the forms are kept as simple and as short as possible:

Listening

> **5** I understood everything the first time. All my answers to the exercises were correct.
>
> **4** I understood almost everything the first time and found it easy after repetition. Almost all my answers were correct.
>
> **3** I understood a lot the first time and almost everything after repetition. I got a few wrong answers.
>
> **2** I understood a lot after repetition but I still have a few doubts. I got several wrong answers.
>
> **1** I found it difficult to understand even after repetition. Most of my answers were wrong.

Writing

> **5** I wrote everything accurately and I made very few errors.
>
> **4** I wrote everything fairly accurately but I made a few errors. However, I can easily correct my errors now.
>
> **3** I made some errors in my writing but there are still a few things which I cannot understand even now.
>
> **2** I made a lot of errors and I still don't understand how to correct most of them.
>
> **1** I was not able to write anything accurately and/or I was not able to finish my written work.

When you use this method of self-evaluation, you can give a more formal questionnaire at the end of the term. This questionnaire will contain questions about the students' achievement in the specific areas covered during the term but it should still be easy for students to complete. Students should be given a space in which to write their answers. There should also be a space for you to write your own comments on each student's answers.

The following example shows you how you can set out your end-of-term questionnaire.

Speaking	STUDENT	TEACHER
1 _____	_____	_____
_____	_____	_____
_____?	_____	_____
_____		

General examples of some questions on speaking and reading which you might include in your questionnaire are:

Speaking

1 What sounds do you still find difficult to pronounce?

2 How often have your teacher(s) and your classmates asked you to repeat what you have said? How often have they been unable to understand you?

3 Which activities this term have you found most difficult? (Say why you found them difficult.)

4 Which activities have been very easy for you?

5 What kind of activities would you like to concentrate on next term?

6 How much has your speaking ability improved this term? (Tick)
No improvement ☐ A little ☐ Quite a lot ☐ Very much ☐

Reading

1 Which books/reading materials have you found most interesting?

2 Which books/reading materials have been most difficult? Why?

3 How difficult have the exercises on the reading material been?

4 How often this term have you read English books and magazines outside the classroom?

5 What kind of books/reading materials would you like to read in class next term?

6 How much has your reading ability improved this term? (Tick)
No improvement ☐ A little ☐ Quite a lot ☐ Very much ☐

It is very useful for students to keep diaries to record the work they have done and the progress they have made. Such learner diaries can then be used to help the students to complete their self-evaluation forms.

Activities

1

Which of the following language skills do you think are better measured by continuous assessment rather than by formal exams?

Using English to solve problems in group work
Obtaining information from a hotel receptionist
Talking in English to other people
Understanding a short paragraph
Recognising the important points in a longer text
Completing a paragraph by putting the correct words in blanks
Understanding the meanings of words from their contexts
Using catalogues in a library to find suitable books
Writing stories
Writing formal letters of complaint

2

Write one or two paragraphs showing why formal end-of-term exams may be unnecessary if a programme of continuous assessment is successful.

3

Design self-evaluation forms which your own students can use for reporting on their performance in reading and speaking. (Note: Do not write questionnaires.)

Discussion

1 Discuss some of the ways in which you could conduct continuous assessment in your school or college.

2 What kind of students in your class would continuous assessment most benefit? Briefly describe these students.

3 What kind of activities in English can best be assessed by means of continuous assessment?

4 To what extent could you use student self-evaluation in your own classes? How could it benefit your teaching? Are there any drawbacks and how best do you think they can be overcome?

Suggestions for further reading

Baker, D 1989 *Language Testing: A Critical Survey and Practical Guide* Edward Arnold

Carroll, B J and Hall, P J 1985 *Make Your Own Language Tests: A Practical Guide to Writing Language Performance Tests* Pergamon

Cohen, A D 1980 *Testing Language Ability in the Classroom* Newbury House, Rowley, Mass.

Finocchiaro, M and Sako, S 1983 *Foreign Language Testing: A Practical Approach* Regents, New York

Harrison, A 1983 *A Language Testing Handbook* Macmillan

Heaton, J B 1988 *Writing English Language Tests* (New Edition) Longman

Heaton, J B (ed.) 1982 *Language Testing* Modern English Publications/Macmillan

Hughes, A and Porter, D (eds.) 1983 *Current Developments in Language Testing* Academic Press

Oller, J W 1979 *Language Tests at School* Longman

Valette, R M 1977 *Modern Language Testing* (Second Edition) Harcourt Brace Jovanovich, New York

Index